# Problem Solving and Reasoning Skills for PEP Maths: NSC Edition

The publishers would like to thank Rising Stars for their kind permission to reproduce the following copyright material:

Trevor Dixon – 9781471880162; 9781471880155

Tim Handley and Paul Wrangles – 9781471885105; 9781471885112; 9781471885099

Tim Handley – 9781783391752; 9781783391769

Tim Handley, Paul Wrangles, Nicki Allman – 9781510403666

Hachette UK's policy is to use papers that are natural, renewable and recyclable products and made from wood grown in well-managed forests and other controlled sources. The logging and manufacturing processes are expected to conform to the environmental regulations of the country of origin.

Orders: please contact Hachette UK Distribution, Hely Hutchinson Centre, Milton Road, Didcot, Oxfordshire, OX11 7HH. Telephone: +44 (0)1235 827827. Email education@hachette.co.uk Lines are open from 9 a.m. to 5 p.m., Monday to Friday. You can also order through our website: www.hoddereducation.co.uk

ISBN: 9781510467644

© Paul Broadbent 2019

First published in 2019 by

Hodder Education,

An Hachette UK Company

Carmelite House

50 Victoria Embankment

London EC4Y 0DZ

www.hoddereducation.com

The authorised representative in the EEA is Hachette Ireland, 8 Castlecourt Centre, Dublin 15, D15 XTP3, Ireland (email: info@hbgi.ie)

Impression number    10 9 8 7 6 5 4 3 2

Year    2025

All rights reserved. Apart from any use permitted under UK copyright law, no part of this publication may be reproduced or transmitted in any form or by any means, electronic or mechanical, including photocopying and recording, or held within any information storage and retrieval system, without permission in writing from the publisher or under licence from the Copyright Licensing Agency Limited. Further details of such licences (for reprographic reproduction) may be obtained from the Copyright Licensing Agency Limited, www.cla.co.uk

Cover artwork by Peter Lubach

Illustrations by Peter Lubach and Aptara Ltd.

Typeset in FS Albert 14/16 pts by Aptara Inc.

Printed by CPI Group (UK) Ltd, Croydon CR0 4YY

A catalogue record for this title is available from the British Library.

# Contents

How to use this book 4
  **1** Hundreds and tens 5
  **2** Exploring numbers 9
  **3** Converting time 13
  **4** Shape and perimeter 17
  **5** Equivalent fractions 21
  **6** Exploring shapes 25
  **7** Multiplication and division facts 29
  **8** Comparing numbers 33
  **9** Money problems 37
**10** Addition and subtraction 41
**11** Lines of symmetry 45
**12** Number sequences 49
**13** Collecting and interpreting data 53
**14** Shapes and lines 57
**15** 24-hour clocks 61
**16** Digits and multiplication 65
**17** Money calculations 69
**18** Multiples 73
**19** Coordinates and shapes 77
**20** Fractions of amounts 81
**21** Symmetrical patterns 85
**22** Number patterns 89
**23** Fractions and money 93
**24** Factors 97
**25** Area of shapes 101
**26** Calculation problems 105
**27** Finding different possibilities 109

# How to use this book

*Problem Solving and Reasoning Skills for PEP Maths* is aligned to Jamaica's National Standards Curriculum. The workbook is designed to systematically develop problem solving and reasoning skills. Learners are encouraged to explore and communicate solutions to everyday scenarios, while teachers/parents are provided with meaningful support to guide learners toward better problem solving and reasoning skills.

First, work through the **Thinking starters** to warm up the problem solving and reasoning skills you already have.

Next, move on to the **Maths mastery** section where you and your classmates can find different solutions to the same situation. It is important to understand that there are many right solutions to problems and many ways of arriving at those solutions.

Afterwards, tackle the **Problem solving** scenario, which tells you the specific reasoning skills that are being developed. Use the prompts in the *Things to think about* box to help you understand the context and find possible solutions. You also get to apply these refreshed skills to an extension activity in the *Your challenge* section. Are your methods and solutions always the same as your classmates'?

Parents/Teachers, **Support notes** on the Maths mastery pages provide practical tips to help you support your learners and the **Tips for success** section provides support for the Problem solving scenario; activity suggestions, extension activities, stimulus questions, suggestions for discussion and space for your own notes. Answers can be found online at www.hoddereducation.com/PEPMaths

# 1 Hundreds and tens

## Thinking starters

**1** Complete these.

a) 7329 = 7000 + ☐ + 20 + ☐

b) 4000 = ☐ tens

**2** Which statements are correct?
Explain your reasoning.

a) 3200 is 32 hundreds.

b) 3200 is 32 tens.

c) 3200 is 3200 ones.

d) 3200 is 320 ones.

**3** Find three different ways to write 7285.

**4** Dan says, '50 + 300 + 4 + 8000 equals 5348.'
Explain to Dan his mistake.

**5** Ben uses blocks like these to show 3-digit numbers.

What is the number closest to 200 that he can make with exactly 8 pieces?

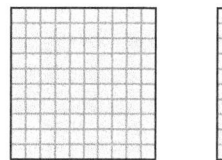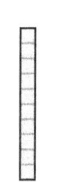

**6** A whole number rounded to the nearest 100 is 6300.

What is the smallest possible number it could be? Explain your reasoning.

# Maths mastery

## Number machine

A machine transforms numbers.

It takes in a number, adds 100, subtracts 10 and then subtracts 100 and spits out the answer.

- If the starting number was 872, what answer will it spit out?
- If the starting number was 704, what answer will it spit out?

The machine spits out the answer 762.

- What number did it start with?

Another machine has a starting number of 412. It is set to find 200 more.

- What number does it spit out?

The machine is changed to find 30 less. The starting number is still 412.

- What number does it now spit out?

Show the method you used to solve the problem. Is it similar to or different from those used by your classmates?

### Support notes

To find 10 more or less than a number, 100 squares can be useful, but for considering 100 more or less, provide children with place-value cards.

They can identify which digits change with each operation. This modelling may also lead children to recognise that the only digit that ends up being altered in the final total is the tens digit (as the +100 and −100 cancel each other out). This is clearer if the whole calculation is shown using a number line.

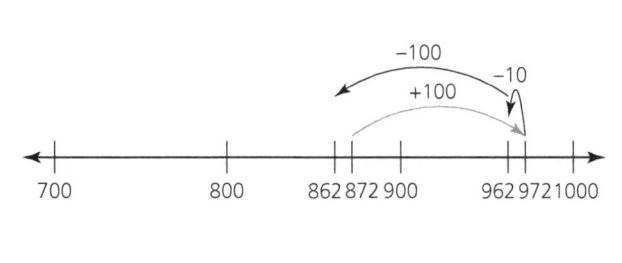

# Problem solving

**Reasoning skills**
- Working systematically
- Finding all possibilities
- Conjecturing and convincing

## Make 100!

This activity is all about trying to make 100, just using the numbers 5 and 10 and the operation of addition.

You could make lots of different numbers, including 100.

For example, you could make 100 by adding:

10 + 10 + 10 + 10 + 10 + 10 + 10 + 10 (or 8 × 10) and 5 + 5 + 5 + 5 (or 4 × 5).

You could also make 100 by using (4 × 10) and (5 × 12) along with many other combinations.

What other pairs of numbers could you use to add together to make 100? For example, could you make 100 using only the numbers 2 and 3? How about 7 and 9? How about 4 and 7?

**Your challenge**

Investigate which pairs of numbers you could combine to make 100.

Are there any pairs of numbers that won't work?

**Things to think about**
- Are there any numbers that you immediately know could combine to make 100? What makes you know that these pairs will work straightaway?
- Do smaller value number pairs have more or fewer possible solutions than larger value number pairs? Why?
- Does it matter if you have an even/odd pairing?
- Can you use your knowledge of multiples of numbers to work out if a pair of numbers could combine to make 100?
- **What do you notice** about the numbers that combine to make 100?
- Give me a **hard and an easy** pair of numbers to prove that they total 100.
- Can you give me a way of using these two numbers to make 100? **Another, another, another**.
- **Convince me** that these numbers do/do not combine to make 100.
- If we know that these two numbers combine to make 100, **what else do we know**?

# Tips for success

Children are asked to investigate which pairs of numbers can be combined to make 100. For example, the numbers 3 and 5 can be combined to make 100 – (3 × 5) + (5 × 17).

In order to solve this problem, children will need to be able to list multiples of each number 1–9.

Multiples are formed by multiplying the number of which you are finding multiples by a whole number.

If children list the multiples of two numbers until they reach 100, they can then look for pairs of numbers that combine to make 100. For example, if investigating the digits 6 and 7:

- **multiples of 6**: 6, 12, 18, 24, 30, 36, 42, 48, 54, 60, 66, 72, 78, 84, 90, 96
- **multiples of 7**: 7, 14, 21, 28, 35, 42, 49, 56, 63, 70, 77, 84, 91, 98

You can then see that 30 (6 × 5) and 70 (7 × 10) both combine to make 100, as do 28 (7 × 4) and 72 (6 × 12).

Children could then work out all possible combinations of numbers 2–10 by listing the multiples of 2–9 and looking for combinations that total 100.

## Try this

### Support

Children will benefit from using a multiplication square to support their identification of multiples. Practical representations such as counters, cubes or number rods may also help to enable children to represent the combination of groups of each number.

### Extension

Children could explore a wider range of numbers, for example, exploring combinations of numbers between 1 and 20. Children could be extended to explore further patterns with multiples of numbers; for example, combinations of three multiples to make 100.

## Progress notes

Please use this space to make your own notes.

# 2 Exploring numbers

## Thinking starters

1 Use these signs for this question. < = >
   Write the correct sign to complete the number sentence.

   a) 99 ☐ 50      b) 45 ☐ 67      c) 150 ☐ 500

   d) 909 ☐ 990    e) 4005 ☐ 670   f) 5003 ☐ 5030

2 Put each set of numbers in order, starting with the largest.

   a) 550   505   595   515   559

   b) 729   702   792   727   712

   c) 191   99    109   119   190

3 Use the digits in these numbers in the sets of three boxes to make a correct number sentence.

   a) 2 5 3   ☐☐☐ > ☐☐☐

   b) 6 1 9   ☐☐☐ > ☐☐☐

   c) 1 6 8   ☐☐☐ > ☐☐☐

4 Find a number for each box so that all the numbers are in order.   61 ☐ 200 ☐ 205 ☐ 413
   Find at least three different ways.

5 Use the digits 4, 3, 8, 5 to make a number that is less than 8000 but greater than 4000.

6 Daniel says all three-digit numbers are equal to or less than 999.
   Do you agree? Use examples to explain your answer.

# Maths mastery

## Duel

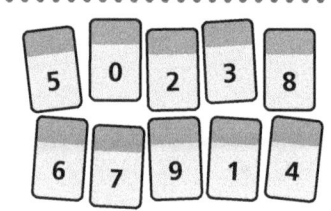

Play a fun game with your partner.

You will need a set of 0–9 digit cards each.

Your challenge is to make the biggest three-digit number you can.

Take it in turns to turn over a digit card and place it in one of the places (hundreds, tens or ones) in your number, telling your partner what value this will have (for example, you could say, 'I am placing my four in the tens place, so it is worth 40').

Keep going until you have turned over three cards each and made your number. When you have placed a digit card, you cannot move it.

- Who makes the biggest number?

Show the method you used to solve the problem. Is it similar to or different from those used by your classmates?

### Support notes

Although this is, to some extent, a game of chance, children should recognise that to make a larger number, they need to place larger digits in the hundreds position and smaller digits in the ones position. Ask them to describe their strategy in order to check whether they understand place value in this way.

Encourage children to consider what makes a number larger than another prior to playing the game. Show them a three-digit number made using digit cards and ask them to make a number that is larger/smaller than it by rearranging the digits.

Give children opportunities to repeat the game several times in order to use their knowledge of place value to try to make the largest number.

# Problem solving

**Reasoning skills**
- Working systematically
- Solving problems

## Terrific thirty-six

Today, my favourite number is 36. I wonder how many different statements and/or questions we could write that have the answer 36?

**Your challenge**

Create as many different statements and/or questions as you can that have the answer 36.

Write five questions that also involve the number 72.

Write some questions in a context.

Write some statements that involve two different operations.

Write a question that involves the < or > sign.

Write some statements that involve a fraction.

Write some statements that involve a decimal.

**Things to think about**
- Can you use any patterns to help you?
- Are there an infinite number of questions and statements that have the answer 36?
- How could you include a fraction or decimal in your questions/statements?
- **What do you notice** about the number 36? This calculation?
- Give me a **hard and an easy** statement/question that has the answer 36.
- Can you give a related statement/question to this one? **Another, another, another**. How are they related?

Show the method you used to solve the problem. Is it similar to or different from those used by your classmates?

# Tips for success

This problem asks children to investigate the number 36, by generating as many different possible questions or statements to which the 'answer' is 36.

This is a combination and extension of the 'If this is the answer, what's the question?' and 'maths stories' key strategies. Children should be encouraged to spot and continue patterns in order to create related questions/statements easily, for example:

2 × 18 = 36        16 × 2.25 = 36
4 × 9  = 36        1 × 36    = 36
8 × 4.5 = 36       0.5 × 72  = 36

Some suggested challenge questions are provided; similar prompt questions can be created as needed. Children can also be encouraged to set each other challenges.

Children should be encouraged to make a wide range of statements, which involve many areas of mathematics. Combined with focused questioning, this activity can therefore provide a very good opportunity for assessment of a wide range of different areas of mathematics.

## Try this

### Support
Working in mixed ability groups, as suggested above, should provide peer support for children who are less confident. Children could also be encouraged to continue simple patterns; for example, they could be provided with the statements 2 + 34 = 36, 3 + 33 = 36, 4 + 32 = 36 and be asked to continue them.

### Extension
Children should be given increasingly more complex challenge questions; for example: *Can you give me a statement that involves a number less than 0.1? Can you give me a question/statement that has two numbers but both of these numbers are the same (for example, 6 × 6 = 36)?*

## Progress notes

Please use this space to make your own notes.

# 3 Converting time

## Thinking starters

1 Answer these.

   a) Maria watches television for 4 hours. How many minutes is this?

   b) Dom ran four laps of a running track. It took him 4 minutes. How many seconds is this?

   c) A teacher said, 'I have worked at this school for 10 years.' How many months is this?

2 Answer these.

   a) How many days are there in 6 weeks?

   b) How many seconds are there in half a minute?

   c) How many hours are there in half a day?

   d) How many days are there in March?

   e) How many seconds are there in 1 hour?

3 Answer these.

   a) A decade is 10 years. A century is 10 decades. How many years are there in a century?

   b) Gabby is changing a number of days into hours. Write the missing number in her calculation.

   144 hours ÷ ☐ = 6 days

   c) Jason says, 'There are exactly 52 weeks in a year.'

   Show that Jason is incorrect.

   d) Manisha leaves work on Friday 5 August to go holiday the next day. She returns on Saturday 20 August. How many days is she on holiday for?

# Maths mastery

## Performance countdown

Class 4 are looking forward to their end-of-term production.
Their teacher tells them it is only 8 days until they perform their first performance.

- How many weeks and days is this?
- How many hours are there until their first performance?
- How many minutes are there until their first performance?

Show the method you used to solve the problem. Is it similar to or different from those used by your classmates?

### Support notes

Encourage children to draw the problem to help. For example, using blocks of time:

| 1 | 1 | 1 | 1 | 1 | 1 | 1 | 1 | days |
|---|---|---|---|---|---|---|---|------|
| 24 | 24 | 24 | 24 | 24 | 24 | 24 | 24 | hours |

× 60  minutes

Discuss with children the different multiplication strategies they could use and help them to choose appropriately.

# Problem solving

**Reasoning skills**
- Working systematically
- Solving problems
- Conjecturing and convincing

## How much time?

There are often news articles about the amount of time children spend in front of 'screens', doing things like playing games, using computers and watching TV.

How much time did you spend in front of a screen yesterday?

How much time will you spend in front of a screen over the next year? Would it be large enough for you to put into weeks? Or even months?

If you put all the times together, how much time is your class likely to spend all together over the next year? Would this be large enough for you to put into years?

**Things to think about**
- How can you convert between different minutes of time? For example, how many minutes are there in an hour? In a day? In a month?
- How are you going to predict your screen time over the next week? Month? Year?
- How is it best to collect all of our screen time together?
- **Convince me** that there are 168 hours in a week.

**Your challenge**

Calculate how much screen time you will spend over the next week, next month and next year.

Can you express this time in the largest time unit possible (days, hours, minutes …)?

What do you find if you put all of the class's screen times together?

# Tips for success

This investigation asks the children to predict how much 'screen time' they will have over the next week, month and year. They are then asked to work out the class's collective screen time and to present it in the largest time unit possible. This will involve the children converting between units of time. They will need to be secure in the knowledge that:

- there are 60 minutes in an hour
- there are 24 hours in a day
- there are 7 days in a week
- there are 52 weeks in a year.

The children should also be able to use these units to convert between other units of time; for example, work out that there are 168 hours in a week.

The calculations involved in converting between units of time should largely be within the ability of a Grade 4 child. However, a calculator could also be used to support calculation skills to maintain the focus on converting between units of time and statistics.

If possible, begin by putting the investigation in context. There are invariably news stories and research published around screen time or what children do in their spare time that could provide a good 'real-life' stimulus. Then show the children the prompt question.

## Try this

### Support
Let children use calculators during the investigative work. Also, they could just focus on the screen time over a week, then move on to four weeks.

### Extension
The children could be challenged to express the screen time in seconds, minutes, hours and, if appropriate, days, weeks and years.

## Progress notes

Please use this space to make your own notes.

# 4 Shape and perimeter

## Thinking starters

**1** Find the perimeters of the rectangles with these lengths and widths.

|    | Length | Width | Perimeter |
|----|--------|-------|-----------|
| a) | 7 cm   | 6 cm  |           |
| b) | 10 cm  | 5 cm  |           |
| c) | 12 cm  | 10 cm |           |
| d) | 20 cm  | 10 cm |           |
| e) | 30 cm  | 20 cm |           |

**2** Answer these.

a) A square has a side length of 8 cm. What is the perimeter of the square?

b) A square has a side length of 20 cm. What is the perimeter of the square?

**3** Each small square on these grids represents a square centimetre. What is the perimeter of each shaded shape?

a)
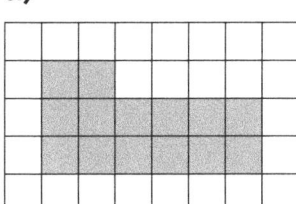

b)
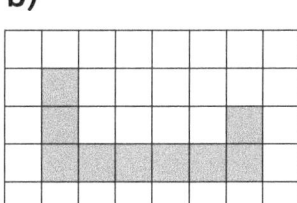

c)
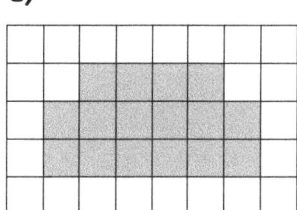

**4** Calculate the perimeter of this shape.

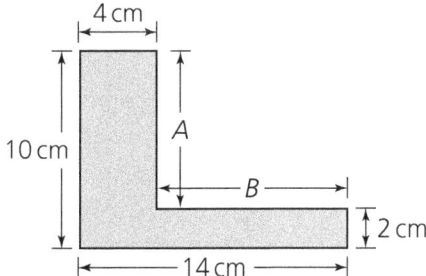

# Maths mastery

## Perimeter puzzle

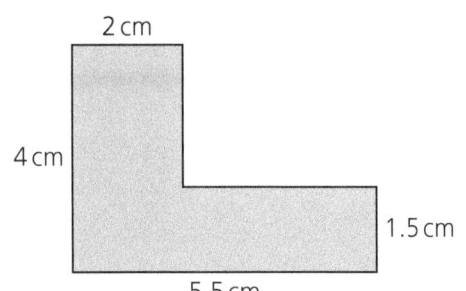

- What is the perimeter of this shape?
- Can you draw a different shape that has the same perimeter?

Show the method you used to solve the problem. Is it similar to or different from those used by your classmates?

**Support notes**

Encourage children to write on a copy of the shape, measuring and labelling each length. Once labelled, children can then add the lengths of the sides to calculate the total perimeter.

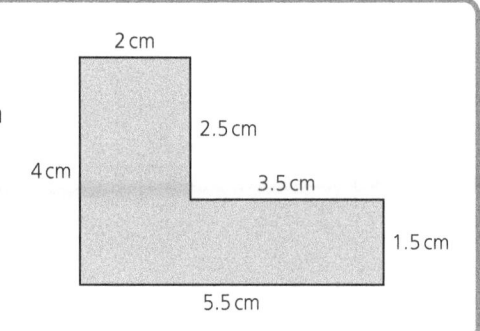

# Problem solving

**Reasoning skills**
- Working systematically
- Solving problems
- Conjecturing and convincing

## Moving and shaping

Your teacher will give you a set of different shapes.

You must arrange the shapes so that they fit together to make one large shape.

Which way of arranging the shapes together would give you the smallest perimeter?

Which way would give you the largest?

You can arrange the shapes in any way you like, but the full sides of the shapes must be touching.

For example, you can have:

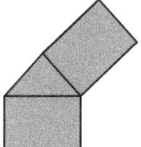

You cannot have:

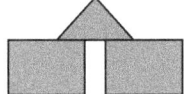

**Your challenge**

Investigate the smallest and largest perimeter that it is possible to make by combining the shapes together.

**Things to think about**
- What rules are you going to set yourself? For example, does the full length of the side of each shape have to touch the side of another shape?
- What type of shapes have the largest perimeter?
- How can you be sure you have found the largest and the smallest possible perimeter?
- If you had another of each shape, how would this affect the largest and smallest perimeters you could make?
- **What do you notice** about the perimeters that give you the larger/smaller perimeters?
- **Convince me** that you have found the largest and smallest perimeter.
- **What is the same? What is different** between your arrangement for the largest and smallest perimeter?
- Give me an arrangement of these shapes that has a larger/smaller perimeter than the shape you have just created. **Another, another, another.**

# Tips for success

The children are asked to work out how to arrange a set of shapes to give the largest and smallest perimeter.

Perimeter is the measure of the distance around a shape or area.

Commercially produced 2-D shapes or 'pattern blocks' can be used, providing the side lengths of these shapes are either full or half units and that they can be placed together.

The children must ensure that sides of the shapes touch fully. Examples of what is and isn't 'allowed' are provided in the problem.

The children can either measure the perimeter of the shapes, or place the shapes on cm² paper to help them calculate the perimeter.

The children are also challenged to consider the impact of adding one more of each shape to the largest and smallest possible perimeters.

They could record their findings by taking photographs of each design or tracing around the edges of their designs. Tablet devices could also be used to photograph and annotate designs.

## Try this

### Support

The children should be encouraged to arrange their shapes on cm² paper to support them in calculating the perimeter. The number of shapes could also be reduced, providing two of two different shapes.

### Extension

The children could be challenged to calculate the area of the shapes they have made. This could be further challenged by specifying that each arrangement of shapes they make must have a value for the perimeter that is greater than the area value.

## Progress notes

Please use this space to make your own notes.

# 5 Equivalent fractions

## Thinking starters

**1** Complete these pairs of equivalent fractions.

a) $\frac{1}{4} = \frac{\square}{8}$

b) $\frac{3}{4} = \frac{6}{\square}$

c) $\frac{2}{4} = \frac{\square}{10}$

d) $\frac{6}{10} = \frac{\square}{10}$

**2** Complete this sequence of equivalent fractions. Look for number patterns.

$$\frac{2}{3} = \frac{4}{6} = \frac{\square}{9} = \frac{8}{\square} = \frac{\square}{15} = \frac{12}{\square}$$

**3** Work out the missing numerators.

a) $\frac{7}{8} = \frac{\square}{24}$

b) $\frac{7}{12} = \frac{\square}{36}$

**4** Answer these.

a) Find three other fractions that are equivalent to $\frac{3}{4}$.

b) Find three other fractions that are equivalent to $\frac{2}{5}$.

# Maths mastery

## Fraction sorting

- Can you sort these images into fractions that represent $\frac{1}{2}$, $\frac{1}{4}$ and $\frac{3}{4}$?

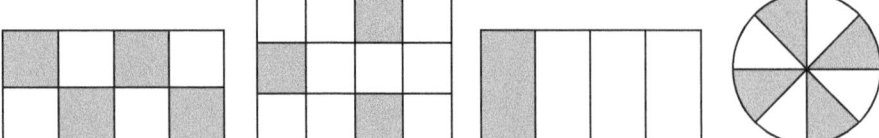

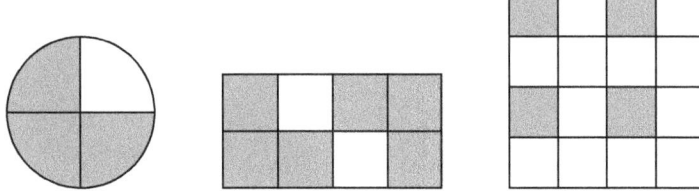

- Can you draw two more images for each group?

Show the method you used to solve the problem. Is it similar to or different from those used by your classmates?

**Support notes**

Remind children of the idea that fractions show '__ out of a possible __'. In these examples, they show '__ shaded out of a possible __'. Provide fraction strips or a fraction wall for children to be able to draw links between equivalent fractions. Most misconceptions around fractions are sorted out when images are drawn to show the fractions.

# Problem solving

**Reasoning skills**
- Working systematically
- Solving problems
- Making connections
- Conjecturing and convincing

## Build a fraction wall

Your teacher will give you some strips of paper.

Fold the strips so that the strips show:

1 whole, $\frac{1}{2}, \frac{1}{4}, \frac{1}{3}, \frac{1}{6}$ and $\frac{1}{8}$.

Put them underneath each other, so that they are all lined up.

**Your challenge**

Can you use the fraction wall that you have just created to work out which fractions are equal (equivalent) to each other?

Can you work out how to find fractions that are equal to each other without using the fraction wall?

**Things to think about**
- What does a fraction actually mean?
- How can you fold your strips to show each fraction?
- How are the different fractions related to each other?
- **What is the same? What is different** between pairs of fractions that are equivalent?
- If we know that $\frac{1}{2}$ and $\frac{2}{4}$ are equivalent **what else do we know?**
- **Convince me** that these fractions are equal to each other.
- Which of these fractions is the **odd one out** and why?
- Give a fraction that is equal to $\frac{1}{4}$. Another, another, another.

# Tips for success

This activity asks the children to fold strips to represent different fractions, in order to create their own fraction wall. Children are then encouraged to use these to make statements about fractions that are equivalent to each other.

In order to do this, children will need to understand that:

- fractions represent a proportion
- a fraction is made up of two parts: a numerator and a denominator
- the denominator shows how many equal parts the whole is split into
- the numerator shows how many of these equal parts are represented/'needed'.

The children need six equally sized strips. The strips are formed by cutting an A4 sheet of paper into strips of paper. Four strips cut lengthways are ideal for this activity.

Children can use the strips folded into quarters to help create eighths, and thirds to help create sixths.

Fractions are equivalent to each other when the numerator and denominator are linked by a common scale factor; for example, $\frac{1}{4}$ and $\frac{3}{12}$ are equivalent as they are linked by a scale factor of 3.

## Try this

### Support

Children should focus on folding strips to show $\frac{1}{2}, \frac{1}{4}$ and $\frac{1}{8}$, and create equivalency statements using these. The children may also find the printed fraction wall useful if they struggle to fold the strips to represent the different fractions.

### Extension

Children should be encouraged to undertake a greater proportion of the challenge independently. Children can also use their fraction wall to explore the addition of fractions.

## Progress notes

Please use this space to make your own notes.

# 6 Exploring shapes

## Thinking starters

**1** These trapeziums are drawn on a square grid.
Tick the trapeziums that have right angles.

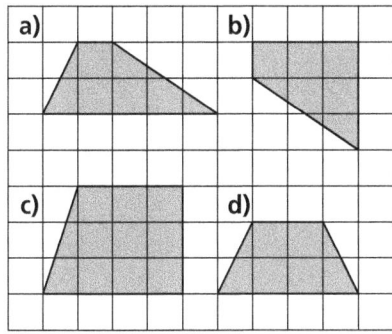

**2** Which of these are isosceles triangles? Tick the answer/s.

a) 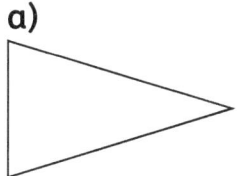   b) 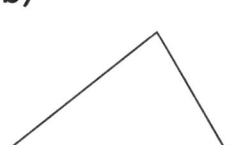   c) 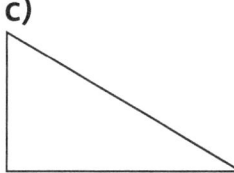   d)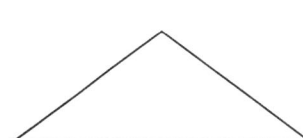

**3** Which of these shapes does not have exactly four sides? Circle the answer/s.

kite            quadrilateral            octagon            trapezium

**4** Which of these shapes do not always have four equal sides? Circle the answer/s.

square          parallelogram          rhombus          kite

**5** Which of these shapes must have right angles? Circle the answer/s.

pentagon          square          rectangle          kite

**6** Write the letters of the obtuse-angled scalene triangles.

a) 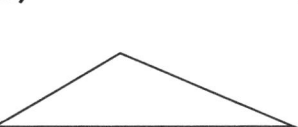   b)    c) 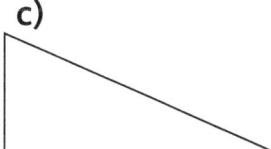   d)

# Maths mastery

## Shape sorting

- Can you help Mina sort these shapes into a Carroll diagram?

|  | All sides are equal | Not all sides are equal |
|---|---|---|
| Has right angles |  |  |
| Has no right angles |  |  |

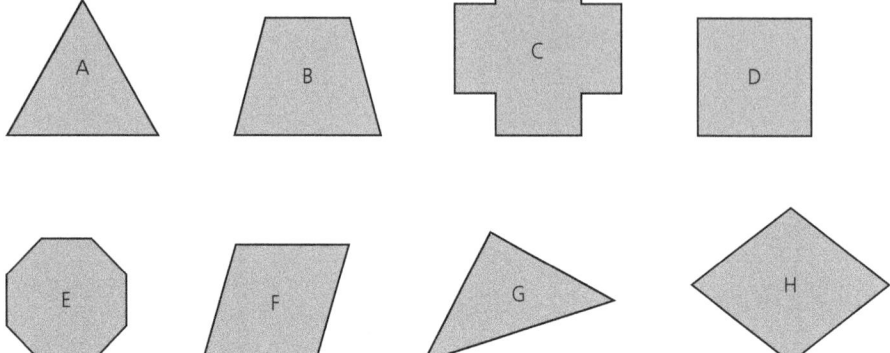

- Can you draw five more shapes and sort them into the correct places in the Carroll diagram?

Show the method you used to solve the problem. Is it similar to or different from those used by your classmates?

**Support notes**
Provide children with square corners, rulers and plastic (or cut-out) 2-D shapes to explore the presence of right angles and equal side lengths on the shapes in the question. They should draw their own Carroll diagram and sort the 2-D shapes physically.

# Problem solving

**Reasoning skills**
- Working systematically
- Solving problems
- Conjecturing and convincing

## Tricky tangrams

A tangram is a traditional Chinese puzzle, made up of seven different pieces.

'Tangram' means 'seven boards of skill'.

Your teacher will give you a sheet with these pieces on to make your own tangram set.

How many different polygons can you make using all seven pieces?

There are lots of different tangram challenges for you to explore!

You could start with the suggestions below.

Ideas to get you started:
- one square
- a right-angled triangle
- two squares that are equal in size.

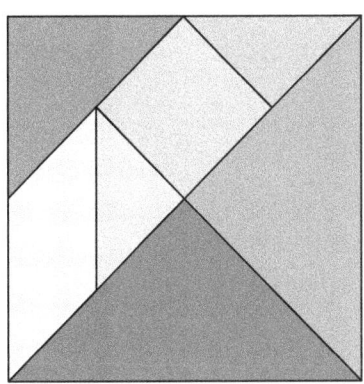

**Things to think about**
- Which pieces fit together well?
- Are there any polygons that you cannot make?
- What are the properties of the different shapes you have made?
- **What do you notice** about the way the shapes arrange together?
- **What is the same? What is different** between (pick two polygons created)?
- Give me another way to make a square (or a different shape). **Another, another, another.**

**Your challenge**
Investigate which different polygons you can make using all seven tangram pieces.

# Tips for success

This problem revolves around the traditional Chinese tangram puzzle.

'Tangram' can be literally translated to mean 'seven boards of skill' with each tangram set made up of seven shapes. The tangram pieces can be assembled to create different shapes. This puzzle challenges children to create as many different polygons as they can, using the tangram pieces.

There are numerous possible solutions. The children should be encouraged to name each polygon they have created and identify some of its properties.

The children should ideally be able to photograph each of their solutions. They could then use a range of different ICT applications to create a poster or slideshow of their solutions.

The problem provides three specific challenges to get children started using their tangram pieces.

## Try this

### Support

The children may find that the three problems will provide enough material for them to work on during the whole lesson. Give children time to work through the activity, working in pairs, encouraging them to name the shape properties of any shapes they create.

### Extension

The children could be asked to investigate the different polygons that are possible to make if they do not have to use all seven pieces.

## Progress notes

Please use this space to make your own notes.

# 7 Multiplication and division facts

## Thinking starters

**1** Write the missing number.

a) $45 \div 5 = \square \times 3$

b) $\square \div 4 = 5 \times 2$

c) $4 \times 2 = 64 \div \square$

d) $\square \div 5 = 4 \times 3$

e) $10 \times \square = 100 \div 10$

**2** The same number is missing in each question. Work out the missing number.

a) $\square \times \square = 36$

b) $\square \times \square = 81$

c) $49 \div \square = \square$

d) $121 \div \square = \square$

**3** Write the missing number.

a) $\square \times 5 = 40$

b) $64 \div \square = 8$

c) $8 \times \square = 56$

d) $\square \div 11 = 9$

e) $4 \times \square = 48$

**4** Find the missing numbers in this multiplication table.

| × |    |    |    |    |
|---|----|----|----|----|
| 5 | 20 | 30 | 15 | 35 |
|   | 32 |    |    |    |
|   |    | 12 |    |    |
|   |    |    | 27 |    |

**5** $4 \times 6 = 24$

Use this fact to answer these questions.

a) $40 \times 6 = \square$

b) $4 \times 600 = \square$

c) $40 \times 60 = \square$

d) $240 \div 60 = \square$

# Maths mastery

## Speedy multiplication

- Can you fill in the missing numbers in this multiplication challenge grid in less than 2 minutes?

| ×  | 12 | 8  |    |
|----|----|----|----|
| 7  | 84 |    | 42 |
| 6  |    | 48 | 36 |
|    |    |    | 54 |
| 3  |    |    |    |

Show the method you used to solve the problem. Is it similar to or different from those used by your classmates?

### Support notes

Provide children with similar problems based on standard multiplication grids to start with (that is, the rows and columns in numerical order).

When approaching this question remove the time constraint and encourage the children to work more slowly until they are at a level to be able to complete the entire grid in less than 2 minutes.

| × | 1 | 2 | 3 | 4  | 5  | 6 |
|---|---|---|---|----|----|---|
| 1 |   |   |   |    |    |   |
| 2 |   | 4 |   |    |    |   |
| 3 |   |   |   |    | 15 |   |
| 4 |   |   |   | 12 |    |   |
| 5 |   |   |   |    |    |   |
| 6 |   |   |   |    |    |   |

# Problem solving

**Reasoning skills**
- Working systematically
- Solving problems
- Conjecturing and convincing

## A dicey game

Can you create a new game a bit like 'Connect 4'?

You will have a grid of numbers, 6 across by 6 down.

To cross off the numbers, you will have to roll two 6-sided dice.

Cross off the product of the values shown on both dice (the answer when you multiply the two dice numbers together; for example, if you roll a 2 and a 4 you could cross off 8).

The first player to cross off three numbers in a row wins.

Your sample grid uses all the numbers 1–36 but it might not be correct.

Can you design another grid for the game?

| 1  | 2  | 3  | 4  | 5  | 6  |
|----|----|----|----|----|----|
| 7  | 8  | 9  | 10 | 11 | 12 |
| 13 | 14 | 15 | 16 | 17 | 18 |
| 19 | 20 | 21 | 22 | 23 | 24 |
| 25 | 26 | 27 | 28 | 29 | 30 |
| 31 | 32 | 33 | 34 | 35 | 36 |

**Your challenge**

Design a grid to use for this new game.

**Things to think about**
- What is the highest number that is possible to make by multiplying two 1–6 dice together?
- How should the numbers be arranged on the grid to make the game fair? Which, if any, numbers should appear twice?
- Are there any numbers that you cannot make?
- Are there any numbers that you are more likely to make?
- How are you going to record your answers?
- How are you going to organise your group so that it works most effectively?
- **What do you notice** about the numbers that you can make by multiplying two faces of a 1–6 dice together?
- **Convince me** that 13 shouldn't be on the grid.
- **Convince me** that 12 should be on the grid more than 36.
- Give me a way you could make 6. **Another, another, another**.

# Tips for success

This investigation asks the children to help design a new game, based on the product of two 1–6 dice faces.

Not all numbers between 1 and 36 are possible to make from the product of two numbers between 1 and 6. Some numbers that are impossible to make are: 11, 13, 14, 17, 19, 22, 23, 26, 27, 28, 29, 31, 32, 33, 34, 35.

## Try this

### Support

The children could use a multiplication square to help them explore this problem, focusing on the 1–6 section.

### Extension

More able children should begin to discuss the second part of the problem much sooner than most children.

They could also extend the activity by using a 1–10 dice together with a 1–6 dice, which gives many more possible products and distributions. Two 1–10 dice can then be used to extend the problem further.

## Progress notes

Please use this space to make your own notes.

# 8 Comparing numbers

## Thinking starters

1 Put this set of numbers in order, starting with the largest.

   6845          6864          7564          7456          6856

2 Here are four digit cards.

   | 4 | 2 | 7 | 8 |

   Use these cards to make:

   a) the largest 4-digit number     b) the smallest 4-digit number

   Explain how you know.

3 Explain how you know that 5734 is greater than 5724 and smaller than 5834.

4 In one of these calculations the missing number is 1000. Explain how you know.

   5894 + ☐ = 5994

   6784 + ☐ = 7884

   3581 + ☐ = 4581

5 8216 can be written as 8200 + 16.

   Find three other ways to write 8216.

6 Here are some digit cards.

   | 5 | 3 | 1 | 9 | 4 |

   Use four of the digit cards to make the 4-digit number that is closest to 5000.

# Maths mastery

## Ordering game

Daniel and Jayden are playing a game where they have to make the biggest possible number out of four digit cards.

Daniel gets the cards 6, 8, 1, 4.
- What is the biggest number he can make?

Jayden gets the cards 7, 3, 2, 6.
- What is the biggest number he can make?
- Can you write a statement using < or > comparing their numbers?
- What is the difference between their numbers?

Show the method you used to solve the problem. Is it similar to or different from those used by your classmates?

### Support notes

Provide children with digit cards and a place-value grid in order to physically manipulate the digits to make the largest possible four-digit numbers. Encourage children to read their numbers aloud or write them in words to check they understand the place value of the numbers they have written.

| Thousands | Hundreds | Tens | Ones |
|---|---|---|---|
| 8 | 6 | 4 | 1 |
| 7 | 6 | 3 | 2 |

Encourage children to consider different ways to find the difference between two numbers (some may choose to count on from 7632 to 8641 rather than using subtraction).

# Problem solving

**Reasoning skills**
- Conjecturing and convincing
- Making generalisations

## Finding the difference

From a set of digit cards containing the digits 1–9, take three cards and arrange them into the biggest number possible; for example, with 4, 5 and 7 you would make 754.

Then using the same three cards, make the smallest number possible, for example 457.

Then find the difference between these two numbers, for example 754 – 457. What do you notice about your answer?

**Your challenge**

Explore what happens when you take the biggest number that it is possible to make out of three digits, from the smallest number.

Are there any rules, patterns or generalisations?

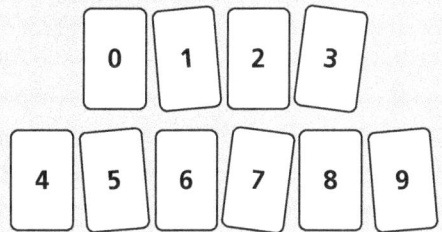

Hint: First, explore the difference between 2-digit numbers and see if anything you notice is the same for 3-digit numbers.

**Things to think about**
- What do you notice about the difference if you use consecutive numbers? (Numbers that follow each other, for example 3, 4, 5.)
- Is there anything that links the differences between your sets of numbers?
- Is there a link? Can you begin to reason why this link may exist?
- **What do you notice** about the results of subtracting these two numbers from each other?
- **Convince me** that your conjecture/generalisation is true.
- **What is the same? What is different** between these two numbers?

# Tips for success

The children are asked to investigate what happens when you subtract a 3-digit number from its reverse; for example, subtracting 678 from 876 (876 – 678 = 198).

To start the activity, ask the children to write down any 3-digit number. Ask them then to write down its reverse and subtract it from their initial number. Then ask children to compare their results with a partner. Ask: *What is the same? What is different?*

When subtracting a 3-digit number from its reverse, the answer is always a multiple of 9.

The explanation is probably beyond Grade 4, but for your information:

Any 3-digit number can be represented as: 100A + 10B + C

The number reversed is: 100C + 10B + A

The difference: (100A + 10B + C) – (100C + 10B + A) = 99A – 99C = 99(A–C)

As the answer is always 99 multiplied by (A–C) and 99 itself is a multiple of 9, then the answer will always be a multiple of 9.

Children should first investigate the difference between a 2-digit number and its reverse. This is also always a multiple of 9. As the result of subtracting the 3-digit number and its reverse is always a multiple of 9, the digit root (keep adding the digits in the number together until you end with a single-digit number) will also always be 9.

As an extra bit of 'maths trivia', if you add the resulting 3-digit number to its reverse, for example 198 + 981 in our example above, the answer will always be 1089, unless the starting number has the same first and third digit.

## Try this

### Support

The children may wish to focus solely on investigating what happens when you subtract a 2-digit number from its reverse.

### Extension

The children can test their generalisations further to see if this extends to 4- or 5-digit numbers.

## Progress notes

Please use this space to make your own notes.

# 9 Money problems

## Thinking starters

1 Bill spent $3.56. Calculate the change he would get from a $20 note.

2 Omar spends $23.78 and pays with two $20 notes.

   Calculate the change he would get.

3 Ben has six coins, which add up to $1.50. What could the six coins be?

4 Ben buys three computer games.

   Game A costs half as much as Game B. Game C costs twice as much as Game B.

   Game B costs $30.

   How much did Ben spend?

5 Harpreet has $30 and wants to buy two T-shirts that cost $7.50 each and two scarves that cost $6.50 each. Does she have enough money?

6 Ben has six notes totalling $80.

   What combination of notes might Ben have?

7 For her birthday, Mia received $10 from her grandma, $25 from her dad and $8 from her friend. How much more money does she need to buy a game she wants that costs $55?

8 Teri says each of these problems can be solved with the calculation 13 × 4.

   Do you agree? Explain your reasoning.

   a) Sam has $13 and then saves $4 more. How much money does he have altogether?

   b) Ravi buys four items, each costing $13. How much does he spend?

# Maths mastery

## Spending power

A shop sells chocolate bars for 45c each, cans of drink for 65c each and raisins for $1.10 for three boxes.

Adam goes to the shop and buys three chocolate bars for 45c each.

- How much change should he get from $2?
- How many boxes of raisins could you buy in the shop for $5?

Zoe buys six boxes of raisins, two cans of drink and a chocolate bar.

- How much change would she get from $10?

Show the method you used to solve the problem. Is it similar to or different from those used by your classmates?

### Support notes

Finding the total of purchases and receiving change after paying is a scenario children will almost certainly have experience of. Provide plastic money for them to tap into their real-life knowledge and role-play the scenario in the question.

# Problem solving

**Reasoning skills**
- Conjecturing and convincing
- Working systematically
- Solving problems

## Disco drinks

Dancing is thirsty work so your next school disco will need a drinks stall.
Imagine that the stall will sell the drinks listed.
Ashley and her four friends each have $1.50 to spend.

## Drinks menu

150 ml cartons of bubble gum flavoured drink (14c each)
200 ml bottles of cherry aid (16c each)
330 ml cans of lemonade (53c each)
500 ml bottles of cola (57c each)
200 ml bottles of limeade (23c each)
200 ml cartons of orange juice (27c each)
200 ml cans of rainbow disco drink (43c each)

**Your challenge**
Work out all the possibilities for:
- what Ashley could buy if she spends all of her money on 4 drinks
- what combinations Riley could buy if he buys more than 6 drinks, but spends all of his money
- what different combinations Jason could buy if he spends 10c on sweets and the rest on drinks – he doesn't like cola
- what Anil could buy if he saved 30c to spend on sweets and buys only two different types of drink
- what combinations Shayla could buy if she ends the night with 7c left.

**Extra challenge**
Can you create your own similar problems for a friend to solve?

**Things to think about**
- Is there more than one possible solution for each challenge?
- Does it matter if the cost of the drinks is odd or even?
- **What do you notice** about the price of the different drinks? Are there any 'good' combinations to use?
- **Convince me** that you have found all the possible solutions.
- Give me a **hard and an easy** question based on the drinks stall. Why is it hard/easy?

# Tips for success

This problem asks children to work systemically to investigate possible combinations that meet a set of criteria.

The problem also involves children calculating with money, including crossing the $1 boundary, a skill with which they should already be secure in Grade 4.

For each challenge there is more than one possible solution.

The prices of the drinks have been set so that they can combine to make multiples of 10c. This is a key element which, once realised, will help in solving the challenge; for example, lemonade (53c) and orange juice (27c) can be combined to make a total spend of 80c.

## Try this

### Support

Children would benefit from using coins to help them represent the values and combinations in this problem.

### Extension

Children could be encouraged to create their own problems, which combine both the price and capacity information provided.

## Progress notes

Please use this space to make your own notes.

# 10 Addition and subtraction

## Thinking starters

1 Answer these. Show your working.
   a) Tom has 56 cards. He buys another 35 but gives 18 to a friend. How many is he left with?

   b) Obe has $100 in the bank. He spends $35 on a computer game and $14 on a T-shirt. How much does he have left?

   c) Leah takes $600 on her holiday. She spends $376 on meals and $175 on gifts. How much does she have left?

2 Answer these. Show your working.
   a) Ayesha plays a computer game. She collects 167 silver rings and 158 gold rings. How many rings does she collect altogether?

   b) Find the total of 515 and 476.

   c) There are 715 workers in a factory and 214 workers in the office. How many workers are there altogether?

3 Answer these. Show your working.
   a) 625 people attend a football match. 414 people stand, the rest have seats. How many have a seat?

   b) A shop has 286 T-shirts. 148 T-shirts are sold. How many are still for sale?

   c) A ship has 2347 passengers. 1463 passengers visit a town. How many passengers are left on board?

# Maths mastery

### What else do you know?

Gabrielle knows that 8 + 7 = 15

Because of this, she says she also knows that 80 + 70 = 150 and 150 − 70 = 80.

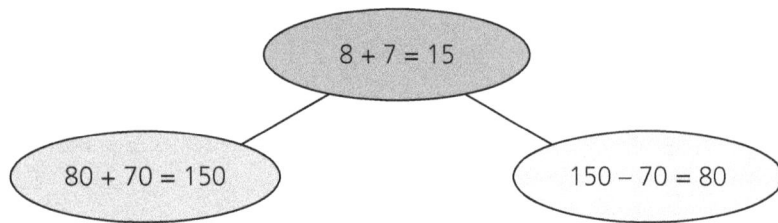

- Can you give eight other number facts that she can easily work out from 8 + 7 = 15?

Show the method you used to solve the problem. Is it similar to or different from those used by your classmates?

**Support notes**

Use base ten apparatus or place-value counters to model the calculation and then encourage children to alter the order, round the numbers and so on to derive related calculations.

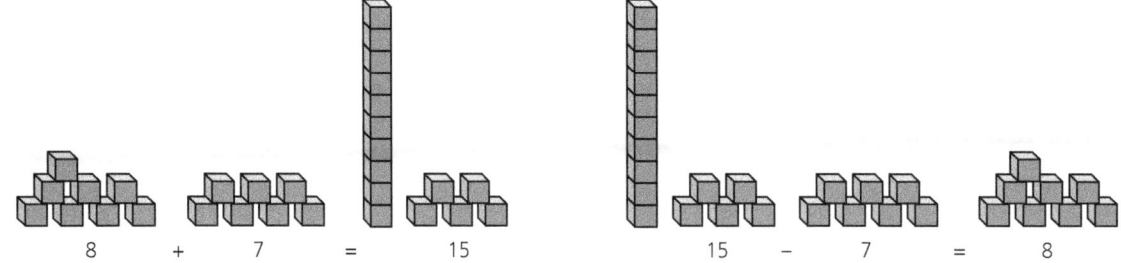

# Problem solving

**Reasoning skills**
- Finding all possibilities
- Working systematically
- Solving problems

## Mystery numbers

Jacob has a set of ten cards with these numbers on:

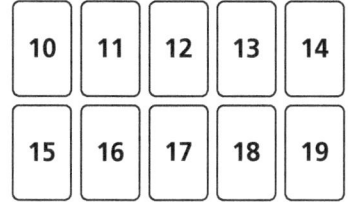

He shuffled the cards and gave two to each of his friends.

His friends told him the sum (total) of the two numbers they were given.

Adam says his cards total 28.

Josh said his cards total 24.

Ellie said her cards total 33.

Dominique said her cards total 34.

Olivia said her cards total 26.

**Your challenge**

Work out which cards each of Jacob's friends are holding.

**Things to think about**
- Is there more than one possible solution?
- Is there more than one way to make each total?
- Do all numbers have the same number of possible ways to make them?
- Would it be easier or harder to solve if I have nine cards and three friends each with three cards? Why?
- **What do you notice** about the number of ways in which you can make each of the numbers?

# Tips for success

This challenge asks children to identify which possible pairs of numbers (from 10–19) could combine to make certain totals. The children need to work systematically in order to solve this problem.

The problem can be solved in many different ways. Children may, however, find it easiest to list all the possible combinations for each number, working systemically by increasing one number while reducing the other, for example:

| 28 | 24 | 33 | 34 | 26 |
|---|---|---|---|---|
| 10 + 18 | 10 + 14 | 19 + 14 | 19 + 15 | 10 + 16 |
| 11 + 17 | 11 + 13 | 18 + 15 | 18 + 16 | 11 + 15 |
| 12 + 16 |  | 17 + 16 |  | 12 + 14 |
| 13 + 15 |  |  |  |  |

The children can then use this information to find sets of cards that do not involve duplicated cards. This leads to there being only one solution.

## Try this

### Support
Use number cards to provide a way for the children to try out different solutions easily and ensure that numbers are not duplicated.

### Extension
The children should progress to creating their own, similar, problems for a partner to solve. They could be challenged to create an 'easy' and 'hard' problem, or one that has more than one possible solution.

## Progress notes

Please use this space to make your own notes.

# 11 Lines of symmetry

## Thinking starters

1 Dotted lines have been drawn on each shape.
  Write the letters of the lines that are lines of symmetry.

   a) rectangle      b) trapezium      c) isosceles triangle

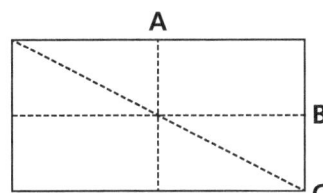 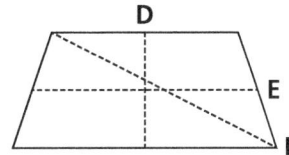 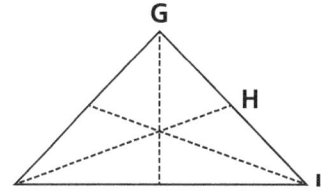

2 These part shapes have been drawn on squared paper. Each dotted line is the line of symmetry of the shape. Complete each shape and name the shapes.

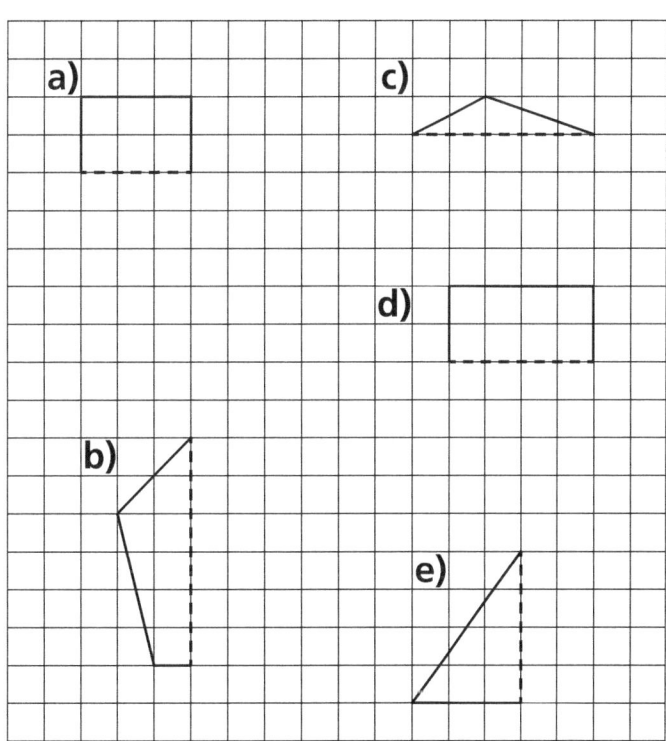

# Maths mastery

## Symmetrical squares

- How many lines of symmetry does each of these patterns have?

  a)          b)          c)

- How can you add one more square to each shape below to give them lines of symmetry? How many lines of symmetry does each shape now have?

  a)          b)          c)

Show the method you used to solve the problem. Is it similar to or different from those used by your classmates?

**Support notes**
Provide children with small mirrors in order to test the lines of symmetry they have identified. Encourage them to cut out their shapes and try folding them along those lines of symmetry.

# Problem solving

**Reasoning skills**
- Finding all possibilities
- Working systematically
- Solving problems

## Crack the code

Shivana has made a 4 × 4 grid on squared paper.
She started to think about how many different symmetrical patterns she could possibly make by shading in some squares on her grid.
For example, she could shade in 4 squares like this to make a symmetrical pattern.

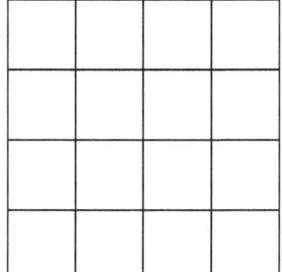 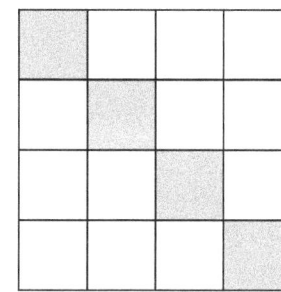

### Your challenge
Find as many different ways as you can of making patterns that have at least one line of reflective symmetry using a 4 × 4 grid.

**Things to think about**
- How many lines of symmetry are there in the unshaded grid? Can you use these to help you identify lines of symmetry when you have shaded different sections?
- How are you going to make sure you have found all possible solutions?
- Is it possible to make a symmetrical pattern by shading an odd number of squares?
- **What do you notice** about the symmetry in this design?
- **What is the same? What is different** between these two solutions?
- Give me a design that uses three shaded squares. **Another, another, another.**
- Which of your designs is the **odd one out?** Why?
- If we know that this design has reflective symmetry, **what else do we know?**

# Tips for success

Children are asked to find all the possible ways to shade a 4 × 4 square so that the square has reflective symmetry. Reflective symmetry is a type of symmetry where one half of an object or pattern is the mirror image of the other half.

Children will need to develop a systematic approach to find all possible designs. For example, they may wish to consider all designs possible when they shade just one square, then all designs possible when shading just two squares, and so on.

Children will need to explore all four lines of reflective symmetry in the square.

Children will need to consider how to best organise their group so that they can find all possible designs. They may, for example, decide that each of them focuses on a different line of symmetry or on a different number of shaded blocks.

## Try this

### Support
Children will benefit from using mirrors in order to check their lines of reflective symmetry. Children may also benefit from being challenged just to find the number of possible designs formed by shading three (or another number) squares.

### Extension
Children can be challenged to find all the possible designs that have two lines of symmetry.

Further work on symmetry could follow this investigation. Children could, for example, investigate symmetry in real life, perhaps through a maths trial. Children could also be challenged to find the lines of reflective symmetry in each letter of the alphabet or in different countries' flags, and so on.

## Progress notes

Please use this space to make your own notes.

# 12 Number sequences

## Thinking starters

1 Circle the term that is the odd one out in each number sequence.

   a)  0, 50, 75, 100, 150, 200, 250

   b)  0, 100, 200, 300, 350, 400, 500

   c)  0, 4, 8, 12, 14, 16, 20

2 Write the missing numbers in the blank squares.

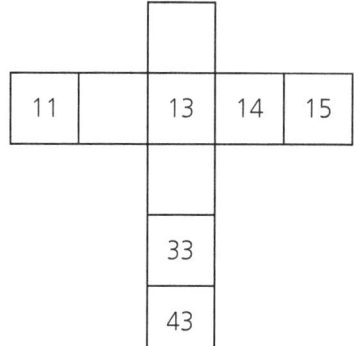

3 These are the first five numbers in a sequence.

| 1st | 2nd | 3rd | 4th | 5th |
|-----|-----|-----|-----|-----|
| 50  | 100 | 150 | 200 | 250 |

Write the 12th number in the sequence.

4 Donna says, 'If I count in steps of 4, the number 60 will be in my number sequence.'
Do you agree? Explain your reasoning.

5 Find the rule for each sequence.

   a)  66, 72, 78, 84, 90 …

   b)  105, 112, 119, 126, 133 …

   c)  325, 350, 375, 400, 425 …

6 Write down the missing numbers in each sequence.

   a) 70, 77, ☐, ☐, 98, 105     b) 225, ☐, ☐, ☐, 325, 350

   c) 36, ☐, ☐, 54, ☐, ☐, 72

# Maths mastery

## Missing numbers

- Can you fill in the missing gaps in the sequences below?

a) | | 6000 | | 8000 | 9000 | | | | 13 000 | |

b) | | 2 | 1 | | | | | −3 | |

Tianna has written a sequence of numbers. She writes:

5500     4500     3500     …

- What is her rule? What are the next five numbers in her sequence?

Show the method you used to solve the problem. Is it similar to or different from those used by your classmates?

### Support notes

As a concrete example for sequence a), use place-value counters to model sequences counting in thousands. Place-value cards can also be useful to demonstrate how the thousands digit is changing each time, as in a Gattegno chart.

| 100 000 | 200 000 | 300 000 | 400 000 | 500 000 | 600 000 | 700 000 | 800 000 | 900 000 |
|---|---|---|---|---|---|---|---|---|
| 10 000 | 20 000 | 30 000 | 40 000 | 50 000 | 60 000 | 70 000 | 80 000 | 90 000 |
| 1 000 | 2 000 | 3 000 | 4 000 | 5 000 | 6 000 | 7 000 | 8 000 | 9 000 |
| 100 | 200 | 300 | 400 | 500 | 600 | 700 | 800 | 900 |
| 10 | 20 | 30 | 40 | 50 | 60 | 70 | 80 | 90 |
| 1 | 2 | 3 | 4 | 5 | 6 | 7 | 8 | 9 |

For sequence b), provide blank number lines (from −10 to 10) to allow children to locate each of the numbers they already know and, from there, to identify the missing numbers and the rule for the sequence.

# Problem solving

**Reasoning skills**
- Conjecturing and convincing
- Working systematically
- Spotting patterns

## Double double

If you started with the number 2 and kept doubling it, you would soon get to a number that is over 100:

2 → 4 → 8 → 16 → 32 → 64 → 128

You could continue this chain and you would soon be over 1000.

Look at the doubling chain. Can you spot any patterns?

Do the patterns exist when you start by doubling another number?

**Your challenge**
Investigate patterns formed by constantly doubling. First, you could investigate patterns that are formed when you start with a single-digit number.

**Things to think about**
- What do you notice about the digits in your double chains?
- Starting with the number 2, you get over 100 after seven doubles. Is this the same for all single-digit numbers? Are there any patterns in how many doubles it takes to get over 100?
- Are all the doubles always even?
- **Convince me** that the pattern you have found exists.
- **What is the same? What is different** between the sequence formed when doubling starting at 2 and 16 (or 3 and 6, 7 and 14, and so on)?
- Give me another starting number that would result in the same sequence. **Another, another, another.**
- Give me a **hard and an easy** starting number. Why are these hard and easy?
- If you know the sequence formed when starting with 2, **what else do you know?**
- **What do you notice** about the number of doubles it takes to get over 100?

# Tips for success

This open-ended investigation essentially asks children: *What do you notice when constantly doubling numbers, starting at different starting points?* It also provides a good opportunity for children to practise their doubling skills. Children should be encouraged to double by partitioning; for example, when doubling 56, double 50 (100) and then 6 (12) before combining (112). Partitioning non-canonically can also sometimes help when doubling; for example, when doubling 63, double 50 (100) before doubling 13 (26) and recombining (126).

Children may first investigate the patterns they notice in the digits that appear in a doubling sequence; for example, when doubling 2 (2, 4, 8, 16, 32, 64, 128 …) the last digits follow the pattern 2, 4, 8, 6, 2 … and when doubling 3 (3, 6, 12, 24, 48, 56 …) the last digits follow the pattern 6, 2, 4, 8, 6 … (apart from 3 itself).

They may also notice that the same numbers appear in the sequences formed when doubling from different starting points. For example, when doubling 2 (2, 4, 8, 16, 32 …), 4 (4, 8, 16, 32 …), 8 (8, 16, 32 …).

Children could also investigate how many doubles it takes to get above a certain number (for example, 100) from different starting points. For example, when starting with 2, it takes seven doubles; when starting with 3 it takes six doubles; when starting with 4 it takes five doubles, and so on.

## Try this

### Support

A range of familiar representations and resources should be provided to support children in the calculation element of this activity. If doubling numbers becomes too challenging beyond 100, children could use a calculator to support the doubling, ensuring the focus remains on the reasoning and making generalisations.

### Extension

The children could be encouraged to explore a wider range of starting numbers, including 3- and 4-digit starting numbers. The children could also be challenged to predict and then work out the number that would be formed by doubling different starting points 15 times; for example, would starting with 4 produce double the answer when starting with 2?

## Progress notes

Please use this space to make your own notes.

# 13 Collecting and interpreting data

## Thinking starters

1. This bar chart shows the numbers of books read by five girls.

   a) How many books did Deb read?

   b) How many more books than Ola did Kim read?

   c) How many fewer books did Deb read than Nia?

   d) How many girls read more than 30 books?

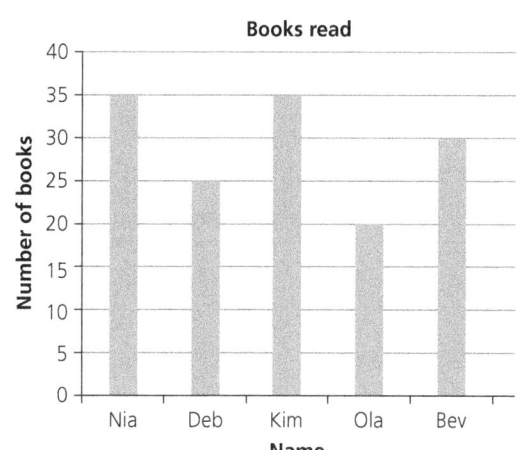

2. This table shows the money raised by five classes for charity.
   Use the information to copy and complete the bar chart.

   | Class | Amount ($) |
   |-------|------------|
   | 1 | 50 |
   | 2 | 30 |
   | 3 | 45 |
   | 4 | 35 |
   | 5 | 40 |

   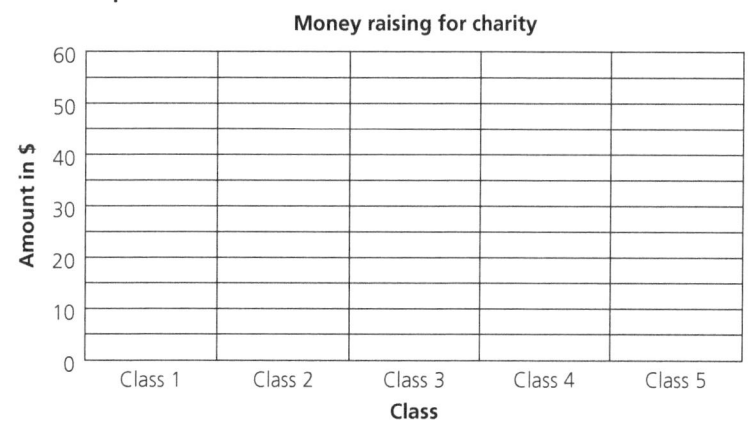

3. Manisha plants a seed and measures the height of the plant each week.

   a) How tall was the plant in Week 4?

   b) How tall was the plant in Week 8?

   c) How long did it take the plant to reach 60 cm?

   d) In Week 6, the plant was 40 cm tall. How long did it take to double in height?

   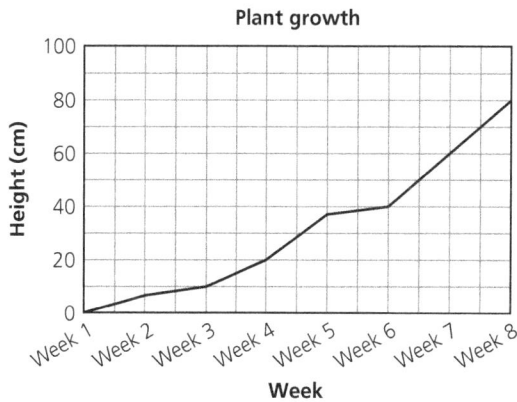

# Maths mastery

### Daily temperatures

Jasmine is plotting a line graph of the outside temperature during a day in March. Her graph is shown below.

At 16:00 it was 8 degrees and at 18:00 it was 6 degrees.

Add these points and complete the line graph.

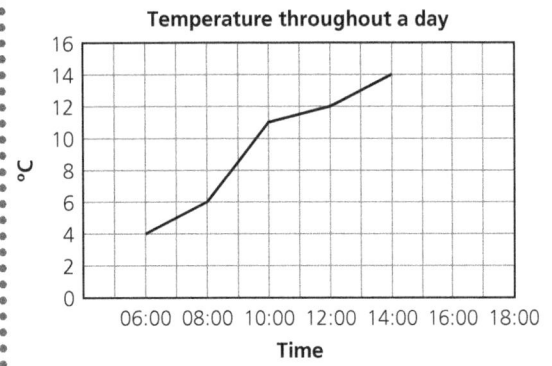

- At what time was the temperature warmest?
- What is the difference in temperature between 08:00 and 14:00?
- Which two times have the biggest difference in temperature between them?
- Can you write three questions about the graph? Try to write at least one that is more difficult to answer than the others. What are the answers?

Show the method you used to solve the problem. Is it similar to or different from those used by your classmates?

### Support notes

Allow children to draw lines up from the x-axis and across to the y-axis (or vice versa) in order to read the information needed. A further useful method is to use right angles (for example, the corner of a piece of paper) to read the graph from axis to axis.

# Problem solving

**Reasoning skills**
- Solving problems
- Making comparisons

## Fastest legs

Mackenzie and Finlay were watching the races at sports day and looked at who won each race.

Finlay said that she thought that the people who won each race were the people with the longest legs.

But Mackenzie thought it depended on more things than this.

I wonder who is right?

### Your challenge

Design, carry out and report on an investigation to find out if people with the longest legs are always, sometimes, or never the fastest runners.

#### Things to think about
- How are you going to carry out this investigation?
- What do you need to measure?
- How many different people do you need to 'investigate' in order to answer the statement?
- How are you going to record and report your results?
- Is the statement **always, sometimes or never true?** Can we say it is always true?
- **Convince me** that this is the most appropriate way to measure/is the most appropriate unit to choose/you are measuring accurately.
- **What do you notice** about the relationship between leg length and running speed?
- **What else do we know** by looking at the data you have collected?

# Tips for success

This problem asks the children to investigate the statement 'Are people with the longest legs, always, sometimes or never the fastest runners?'

The children will need to decide how to carry out this investigation. They should ideally measure the leg length of a range of different people in the class, then time them running over a set distance and then compare the results.

The results of this investigation are best presented in a table, comparing leg length to time over the set distance. You may also wish to take the data and, using ICT, present on a scatter graph to illustrate how the data could also be presented.

The investigation could also be carried out as a whole class, with the children working in pairs to measure leg length and running time, before collating the results together.

Through the investigation, children should focus on choosing appropriate units of measure and taking accurate measurements.

## Try this

### Support
The mixed-ability grouping in this activity should provide peer scaffolding for children. Panic envelopes could also be used, providing different hints/tips for carrying out the investigation.

### Extension
The children could extend this investigation to investigate the effects of other factors, for example age or overall height, on running speed.

## Progress notes

Please use this space to make your own notes.

# 14 Shapes and lines

## Thinking starters

1 How many pairs of parallel lines are there in each shape?

   a)    b)    c)    d)

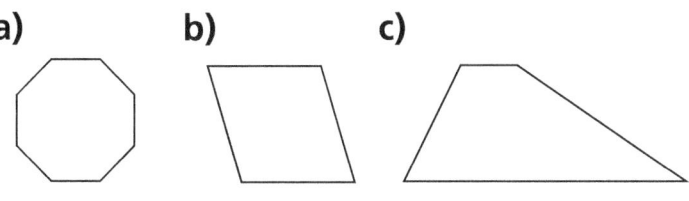

2 Draw these shapes.
   a) A shape with four pairs of perpendicular lines.

   b) A shape with three pairs of parallel lines.

3 Ned says, 'This shape cannot be a square because it does not have any horizontal or vertical lines.'
   Is Ned correct? Explain your answer.

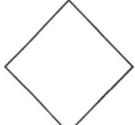

4 Samir says, 'Triangles can have angles that are larger than a right angle.'
   Is Samir correct? Explain your answer.

5 A rhombus is a quadrilateral with four equal sides.
   Explain whether a rhombus is a regular or an irregular shape.

6 Are these statements always, sometimes or never true?
   a) The diagonals of a square meet at right angles.

   b) The diagonals of a rectangle meet at right angles.

# Maths mastery

## Surface shapes

- Can you help Robert sort these shapes into this Venn diagram?

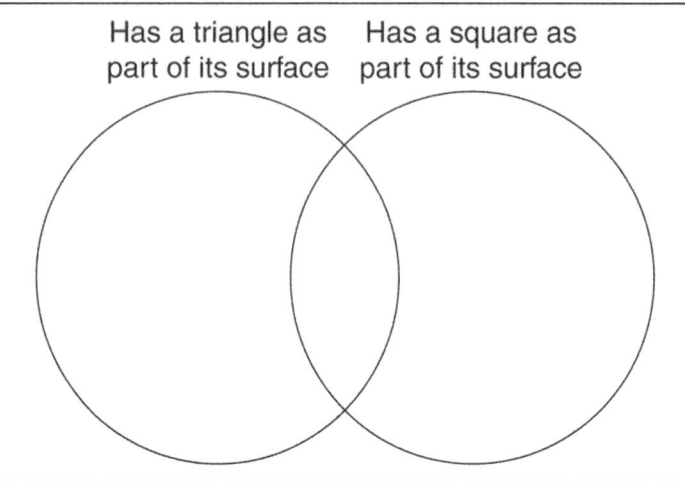

A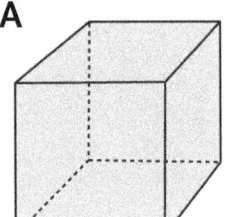

B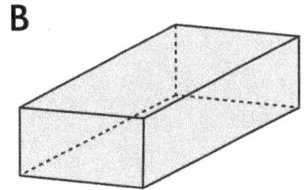

C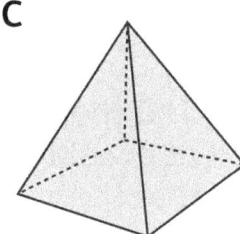

D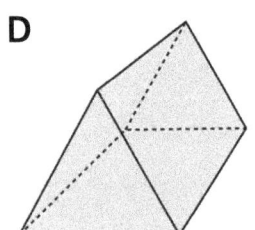

E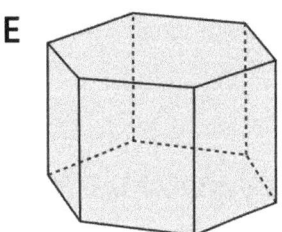

F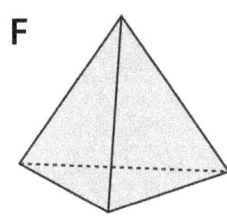

### Support notes

Identify the different possible 3-D shapes that have triangular or square faces by examining plastic 3-D shapes. Discuss the names of each shape and use hoops on the floor or draw circles on a large piece of paper to practise physically sorting the shapes into a Venn diagram.

To go into greater depth, provide children with a collection of different 3-D shapes. They should design a Venn diagram where the shapes are sorted according to different properties. Ask: *Why have you placed this shape here?* Children should refer to their properties.

# Problem solving

**Reasoning skills**
- Finding all possibilities
- Working systematically
- Making comparisons

## Cutting the grass

The Best Bay Hotel has a perfect square lawn in front of the main entrance. The hotel recently employed a new gardener and he has come up with an idea to make the lawn a little more interesting.

The gardener decides to use a lawn mower to make straight lines that cut the whole lawn in half. He starts by cutting a single diagonal line and it splits the square into two triangles.

The hotel guests are impressed. Are there any other shapes the gardener could make by mowing a single line across the square?

> **Your challenge**
> Investigate the different shapes that can be made by mowing one, two, three or four lines across the square lawn. Each of the lines must cut the square in half.

**Things to think about**
- How many different ways are there to cut a square in half? (These are the different routes across the lawn that the lawn mower can take.)
- How can you be sure that you have found all the different possibilities?
- As well as trying to give each shape a name, think about what its properties are.
- Give me an **example** of a way to split the square using two lines. What shapes do you make?
- **What do you notice** about every single shape you make?
- Do the lines **always, sometimes or never** split the square into equal shapes?
- Can you find a way to make two different sizes of triangles? **What is the same? What is different** about them?

# Tips for success

Children investigate the different shapes made when lines are drawn, bisecting a square. Children consider the different ways of drawing lines across a square so that it is split in half (there are four possibilities: a horizontal line halfway down, a vertical line halfway across and two diagonal lines). These are the only lines children can draw. They then consider different combinations of these lines and the shapes that are created as a result.

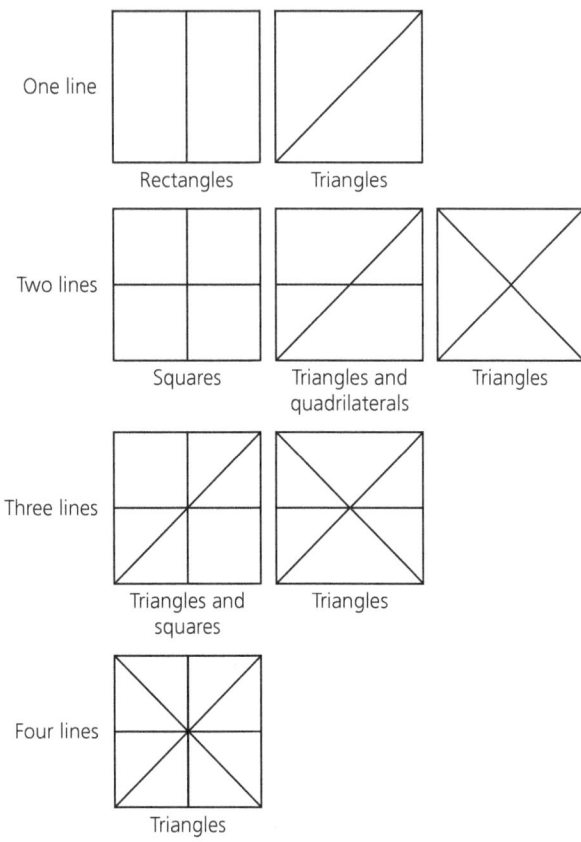

Although the only lines children draw are those that would bisect a square, it is important that they do not think that the shapes created show halves, quarters and so on. Some combination of lines will, others will not.

## Try this

### Support

Give children squares of paper to fold three times. After folding, ask them to cut along each fold to compare the different shapes they have made. They could sort the shapes into sorting circles. Being able to rotate and flip shapes will allow children to see their similarities much more clearly.

### Extension

Ask children to consider the shapes that can be made on a pentagonal (regular) lawn with different cuts.

Use the idea of looking down on a shape to consider symmetry and lines of symmetry in different 2-D designs. For example, ask children to design a square flower bed for the hotel so that it has two lines of symmetry when you look down on it.

# 15 24-hour clocks

## Thinking starters

1 For each clock, write the time in:
   i) words
   ii) 24-hour time.

   a) In the morning

   b) In the afternoon

   c) At night

2 Write these 12-hour times in:
   i) words
   ii) 24-hour time.
   
   a) 6:45 a.m.
   b) 9:25 p.m.
   c) 2:40 a.m.

3 Ben checks a timetable. His train leaves at 14:50.
  Ben says, 'I thought my train left at 2:50 p.m.' What do you think about what Ben has said?

4 Obe checks the time. It is 23:45. Obe says, 'It will be 24:15 in half an hour.'
  Explain Obe's mistake.

5 The time is 16:35. Bess says, 'It is closer to 4 p.m. than it is to 5 p.m.'
  Explain if Bess is correct or not.

6 Find a 24-hour time in which the digits used total 15.

# Maths mastery

## Shopping times

In the shopping centre near Anil's house there is a wall that has three clocks on it: an analogue clock, a 12-hour digital clock and a 24-hour digital clock. All the clocks show the same time.

During the day, Anil passes these clocks three times.

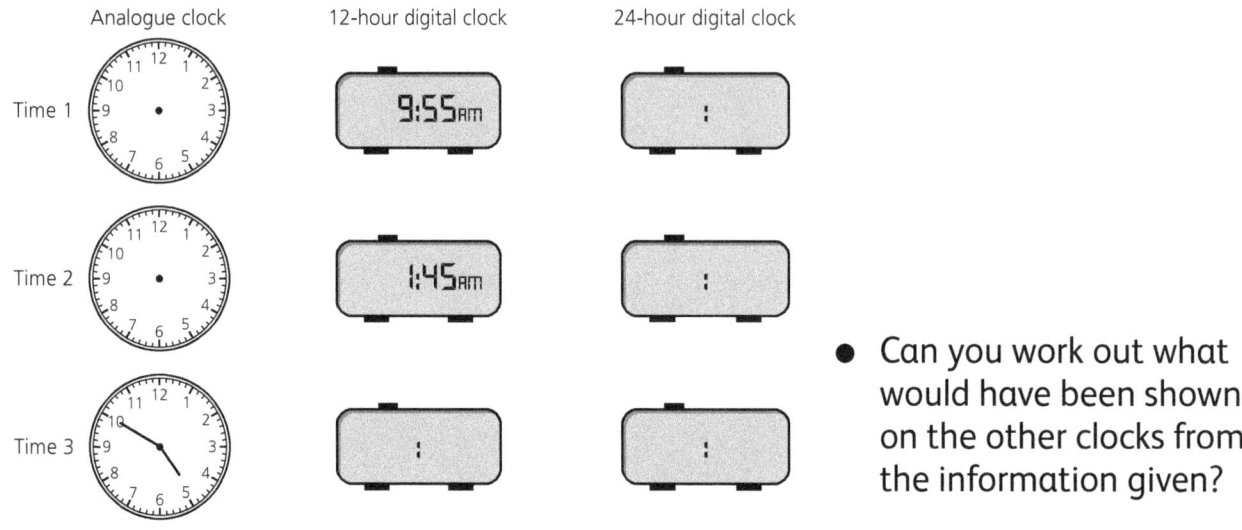

- Can you work out what would have been shown on the other clocks from the information given?

Show the method you used to solve the problem. Is it similar to or different from those used by your classmates?

### Support notes

Children can use analogue and digital clocks to model the different times shown. Geared teaching clocks would be useful when considering how the hour hand moves on an analogue clock.

They should be able to explain the connection between analogue clocks and 12- and 24-hour clock times.

Ask children to devise a set of rules that will help others to read and convert times shown in different ways. Ask: *How do you know whether a time is in the morning or afternoon? How do you know how to write or read a 24-hour clock time?*

# Problem solving

**Reasoning skills**
- Finding all possibilities
- Working systematically
- Using numerical reasoning
- Convincing

## Patterns on digital clocks

Jack looks at his digital clock next to his bed.

It reads: 11:11:11

He knows that, using the 24-hour clock, the time is 11 minutes and 11 seconds past 11 a.m.

Jack thinks, 'I wonder how many times the digit 1 appears on a digital clock over a 24-hour period?'

**Your challenge**

Identify how many times the digit 1 appears in the time on a digital clock, using hours, minutes and seconds, over 24 hours.

**Things to think about**
- Think about how often the numbers change in the seconds, minutes and hours.
- What patterns do you see? Are they always repeated?
- Make sure you are systematic in your recording – you don't want to miss one!
- If the digit 1 appears 16 times in the seconds, in each minute, **what else do we know?**
- **What do you notice** about the results for seconds and the results for minutes?
- **What is the same? What is different** about the results for hours and minutes/minutes and seconds?
- **What is the link** between the patterns found in each hour within a 24-hour period?

# Tips for success

Children investigate how many times the number 1 appears on a digital clock in 24 hours, using the 24-hour clock format and hours, minutes and seconds.

Children will need prior experience of working with time and telling the time. They will need to know how digital clocks show the time and how time is displayed using the 24-hour clock.

This activity will enable children to practise using the vocabulary of time, including the units and how they relate to each other:

>1 minute = 60 seconds, 1 hour = 60 minutes, 1 day = 24 hours.

It is important that children are encouraged to work systematically and make connections; for example, working out how many times the 1 appears in the seconds digits within a minute and then multiplying this by 60 for each minute within an hour, then finding out how many times the 1 appears in the minutes digits within an hour and multiplying this by 24, and then finally focusing on how many times the 1 appears in the hours digits.

## Try this

### Support

Initially restrict the problem to finding out how many times the digit 1 appears between 10:00:00 and 11:00:00. Then extend the problem, encouraging children to make connections between the number of 1s that appear within the seconds and minutes times in each hour.

### Extension

Children explore what other patterns they can spot on digital clocks over a 24-hour period. Ask children to work in pairs to create a different problem for another pair to solve; for example, how many times are there only two different digits on the display (for example, 12:12:12) or how many times are there where one digit is repeated five times (for example, 14:44:44)?

To take it further, ask children to investigate whether they would get the same answer if they were using the 12-hour clock over a 24-hour period and explore which elements of their working and solution to this problem would stay the same and which would be different.

## Progress notes

Please use this space to make your own notes.

# 16 Digits and multiplication

## Thinking starters

1 Complete these calculations.

 a) $20 \times 1 = \square$  b) $12 \div 1 = \square$

 c) $7 \square 6 = \square \times 7$  d) $16 \times 6 = \square$

 e) $96 \div 6 = \square$  f) $70 \div 7 = \square \div 5$

2 Complete these.

 a) $6 \times \square = 36$  b) $60 \times \square = 360$

 c) $600 \times \square = 3600$  d) $6000 \times \square = 36\,000$

3 Find three pairs of numbers that multiply to give 24.

4 What could the missing numbers in this number sentence be?

 $18 \times 8 = 18 \times 2 \times \square \times \square$

5 Find the missing numbers.

 a) $6 \times 7 = 5 \times 7 + \square$  b) $6 \times 7 = 4 \times 7 + \square$

 c) $6 \times 7 = 3 \times 7 + \square$  d) $6 \times 7 = 2 \times 7 + \square$

6 Find the missing numbers.

 a) $\square \div 5 = 1$

 b) $\square \div 5 = 10$

 c) $\square \div 5 = 100$

 d) $\square \div 5 = 1000$

# Maths mastery

**Digit card options**

Mia has three digit cards.
- How many different two-digit numbers could she make out of these cards?

Jacob has seven times as many digit cards as Mia.
- How many cards do they have altogether?

Show the method you used to solve the problem. Is it similar to or different from those used by your classmates?

**Support notes**
Use digit cards or pieces of paper with the digits written on for the three digits and physically place them beside each other to make two-digit numbers. For the second part of the question use more pieces of paper or counters, if necessary, to model what is happening.

# Problem solving

**Reasoning skills**
- Finding all possibilities
- Working systematically
- Using numerical reasoning
- Spotting patterns and relationships

## The curious postman

Bob is a postman. He's really curious about numbers.

As he looks at each house number, he tries to discover patterns and interesting facts about them.

One day, he looks at house number 18. He thinks to himself, 'That's curious!'

'1 + 8 makes 9,' he says. 'And 9 fits into 18 twice. That means that the number 18 is twice its digit sum:

2 × (1 + 8) = 18'

### Your challenge

Explore different 2-digit numbers that Bob might also be interested in. Look for numbers that are twice (or three times, four times and so on) their digit sum. How many can you find?

### Things to think about
- What does it mean to find the 'digit sum'?
- Can you think of a number where the digit sum is 6?
- Is the digit sum always a factor of the number itself? Can you spot any patterns?
- Give me an **example** of a number that can be divided by the sum of its digits.
- 42, 44, 48, 50: which is the **odd one out?** Why?
- Is it **always, sometimes or never true** that, when you add a number's digits together, the resulting number will divide into the original number?
- If the sum of its digits is 4, **what is the number?** If the sum of its digits is 4 and it divides by 4, what is the number?

# Tips for success

Children investigate the links between the digit sum and the number itself. They identify whether a 2-digit number can be found by multiplying its digit sum by another whole number.

The digit sum is the total found by adding the number's digits together; for example, the digit sum of 35 is 8 because 3 + 5 = 8.

Some numbers can be made by multiplying the digit sum by another whole number. For example, the digit sum of 12 is 3 (1 + 2 = 3) and four times this amount makes the number itself (4 × (1 + 2) = 12); the number 12 is four times its digit sum.

The 2-digit numbers that have a link between the digit sum and the number itself are 10, 18, 20, 21, 24, 27, 30, 36, 40, 42, 45, 48, 50, 54, 60, 63, 70, 72, 80, 81, 84 and 90. Children may be able to reason numerically why some of these numbers feature. For example, the multiples of 9 always have a digit sum of 9, so any of the multiples can be found by multiplying 9 by a whole number. The multiples of 10 are the result of multiplying a digit by 10; that digit is always in the tens place next to a 0 (so the sum will be equal to the digit itself).

## Try this

### Support
Encourage children to work through the 2-digit numbers from 10 systematically, as the lower numbers are easier to work with. Ask children to make each number with digit cards, then place them into a scaffolded sentence: __ + __ = __ (for example, the digits in 12 could make 1 + 2 = 3).

Children then arrange manipulatives in groups equal to the total of the digits (in this case, groups of 3) and try to make their original 2-digit number.

### Extension
Encourage children to consider whether there are any 3-digit numbers that meet this rule. Consider how adding an extra digit (the 1 in the hundreds place) might affect any answers they found when thinking about 2-digit numbers.

There are many patterns involving digits of multiples of numbers and digit sums. Use the opportunity to investigate these further. For example, the sum of the digits of multiples of 3 always makes 3, 6 or 9. Encourage children to consider what happens when a total is a 2-digit number itself (they find the digital root by adding the digits together until they have a 1-digit answer).

## Progress notes

Please use this space to make your own notes.

# 17 Money calculations

## Thinking starters

**1** Circle the correct answer for each of these.

a) What is the total cost of three tickets at $35 each?

$95        $105        $85

b) What change from $50 is there for a toy costing $37.60?

$23.40        $13.40        $12.40

c) A bag costs $85 and a purse costs $47. What is the total cost?

$122        $132        $112

d) Two items cost a total of $28.50. If one of the items costs $19.80, what is the cost of the other item?

$9.70        $9.30        $8.70

**2** Complete the missing prices on this chart.

| Item | Cost of 1 | Cost of 2 | Cost of 3 | Cost of 4 | Cost of 5 |
|------|-----------|-----------|-----------|-----------|-----------|
|      | $14       |           |           |           | $70       |
|      | $60       |           | $180      |           |           |
|      | $120      |           |           | $480      |           |
|      | $200      |           |           |           | $1000     |

**3** On a trip to a bird sanctuary, Ali bought six postcards costing 90c and some posters costing $1.20. The total cost was exactly $9.
How many posters did he buy?

**4** Ali sent a birthday card to his friend. It cost 55c to post.
He stuck on eight stamps. Each stamp was either 10c or 5c.
How many of each stamp did he stick on his parcel?

# Maths mastery

## Shopping

Gena visits her local shop. She sees these things for sale.

She buys a magazine and a chocolate bar and pays with a $5 coin.

- How much change does she get?

Jayden visits the same shop and buys a magazine and a can of drink. He pays with two $1 coins.

- What is the fewest number of coins Jayden could receive in his change?

Another shop sells the following products:

loaf of bread – 80c           magazine – $1.10

chocolate bar – 65c         ready meals – $3.50

can of orangeade – 70c

Shaun buys two chocolate bars and a can of orangeade and pays for it with a $5 coin.

Holly buys two ready meals and a loaf of bread and pays for it with a $10 coin.

- Who has the most change?

Show the method you used to solve the problem. Is it similar to or different from those used by your classmates?

**Support notes**

Finding the total of purchases and receiving change after paying is a scenario children will almost certainly have experience of. Provide plastic money for them to relate to their real-life knowledge and model the scenario in the question.

# Problem solving

**Reasoning skills**
- Finding all possibilities
- Working systematically
- Using numerical reasoning

## A day in the life of a parking space

Su Sookey is a car park attendant. Her job is to ensure the smooth running of a multi-storey car park.

One day, Su thinks about how much money the car park is making. She watches one parking space and works out how much money it could earn in 12 hours.

For example, a car parking for 6 hours and two cars each parking for 3 hours would make $19.50 ($10 + $4.75 + $4.75).

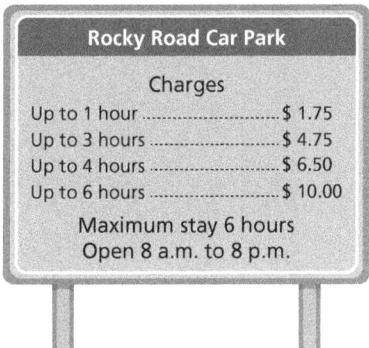

**Rocky Road Car Park**

Charges
Up to 1 hour .......................... $ 1.75
Up to 3 hours ........................ $ 4.75
Up to 4 hours ........................ $ 6.50
Up to 6 hours ........................ $ 10.00

Maximum stay 6 hours
Open 8 a.m. to 8 p.m.

**Your challenge**

What are the different amounts that one parking space could earn in a day?

**Things to think about**
- How can the parking space make the most amount of money?
- How can the parking space make the least amount of money?
- Is there a way to work systematically to find all the possibilities?
- Suggest a way that the parking space could be used during the 12 hours it is open. **Another, another, another.**
- **Convince me** that you have found all the possible amounts the parking space can 'earn' in 12 hours.
- **What do you notice** about the different ways the parking space could be used?
- Is this investigation a good **example** of finding different ways to make 12?

# Tips for success

In this activity, children investigate the total amount of money a parking space can 'earn' during a 12-hour day.

The activity will help children to practise vocabulary associated with money (dollar, cents, total) as well as to practise the skill of adding money written in decimal form.

Each parking ticket lasts for 1, 3, 4 or 6 hours. Therefore, children must find as many different combinations of 1, 3, 4 and 6 that equal 12 as possible (for example, 6 + 6, 6 + 4 + 1 + 1 and so on).

They must then find the cost of the parking tickets for each combination.

Remind children that they are investigating the amount of money that is spent on tickets, rather than a particular sequence of numbers. So, if a car stays in the space for 3 hours, then another car for 6 hours and a final car stays there for 3 hours, this will yield the same amount of money as if the order was different (6, then 3, then 3, for example).

For the purpose of the activity, presume that each car stays the full length of its ticket time.

## Try this

### Support

Encourage children to record the possibilities visually. For example, ask them to make towers of 12 cubes out of smaller towers of 1, 3, 4 and 6 cubes. How many different combinations can they use? Provide children with a simplified version of the problem with the car park prices altered to $1.50, $4.50, $6.50 and $10.

### Extension

Ask children to tackle this problem: Su has decided to open the car park for 6 more hours. The new opening times are 6 a.m. to midnight. How much more money could each space make?

## Progress notes

Please use this space to make your own notes.

# 18 Multiples

## Thinking starters

1. Write the rule for each set of multiples.
   a) 40, 44, 48, 52, 56 …
   b) 48, 56, 64, 72, 80 …
   c) 200, 250, 300, 350, 400 …

2. Write down the missing numbers in each set of multiples.
   a) 50, ☐, 70, ☐, 90, ☐
   b) 200, ☐, ☐, 500, ☐, 700
   c) 16, ☐, 32, 40, ☐, ☐, 64
   d) 16, ☐, 24, ☐, ☐, ☐, 40

3. Here are five numbers.
   36   34   42   30   24
   a) Write the four multiples of six in order, starting with the lowest.
   b) What is the next multiple of 6?

4. Answer these.
   a) Write the fifth multiple of 7 after 21.
   b) Write the sixth multiple of 9 after 54.

5. Explain how you know that 5175 is a multiple of 25.

6. A set of multiples of 7 starts at 7. Write the 15th multiple.

7. Ben counts on in 7s:
   114, 121, 128, 135, 142
   Explain how you can tell that these are not multiples of 7.

8. Nia counts on in multiples of 9:
   342, 351, 362, 369
   Which number is incorrect? Explain your answer.

# Maths mastery

## Counting in multiples

Children in Maple class make the following statements about multiples of numbers.

78 is a multiple of 6

108 is a multiple of 9

152 is a multiple of 7

350 is a multiple of 25

Jacinta        Leo        Marlon        Maria

- Which children are correct? How do you know?

Marlon has a 100 square in front of him. He puts a yellow counter on every multiple of 6, a blue counter on every multiple of 7, a green counter on every multiple of 9 and a red counter on every multiple of 25.

- Which of these squares will have more than one counter on them: 18, 45, 75 or 84?
- Which colours will the counters be?
- Find a number greater than 100 that would have two or more counters on it.

### Support notes

Discuss the properties of multiples (for example, multiples of 6 are always even, they are also multiples of 3 and so the digits add up to a multiple of 3). Provide children with empty number lines for them to record how to start counting on from a number they already know (for example, 25 × 10 = 250 and 350 is only another four lots of 25 on).

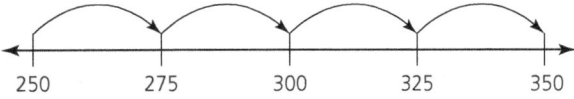

Encourage them to get as close to their target number as possible, modelling it on the number line, before counting on (for example, if children know that 10 × 7 = 70, they can use this to find 20 × 7 = 140, which is close to 153, and they can count on from there).

# Problem solving

**Reasoning skills**
- Spotting patterns and relationships
- Working systematically
- Using numerical reasoning

## The search continues for the perfect planet!

The crew of a spaceship is hunting for the perfect planet. There are hundreds of possible planets for the spaceship to visit. They all have a different number, from 1 onwards.

There are nine features the astronauts need to consider:

1 Every second planet has clean air.
2 Every third planet has gravity similar to Earth.
3 Every fourth planet has an excellent landing spot.
4 Every fifth planet has water.
5 Every sixth planet has a natural food supply.
6 Every seventh planet has a climate like Earth's.
7 Every eighth planet has evidence of life.
8 Every ninth planet has its own natural resources.
9 Every tenth planet is just the right temperature.

**Things to think about**
- What strategies can you use to count in twos, threes, fours, fives, sixes, sevens, eights, nines and tens? Are any of these related?
- How will you record your results?
- Do you think any planet number will have all nine features? What sort of number would you expect a perfect planet to be?
- Give me a number you would say if you were counting in sixes. **Another, another, another.**
- **What do you notice** about the planets you would want to avoid?
- **Convince me** of the next planet number to have six or more factors.
- What is the **quickest or easiest** way to find a number that is a multiple of 2, 3, 4, 5, 6, 7, 8, 9 and 10? Are any of these multiples related?

**Your challenge**

Which planets have none of the features the crew is looking for?

Will the spaceship crew have to settle for a planet with several of the features, but not all?

How close to a perfect planet can you get?

# Tips for success

This problem is explored as a spaceship crew searching for the perfect planet, counting in steps of 2, 3, 4, 5, 6, 7, 8, 9 and 10 and also considering numbers that are multiples of as many of the numbers 2 to 10 as possible.

Children count in multiples of 2, 3, 4, 5, 6, 7, 8, 9 and 10 to see which numbers occur in each count (in particular, which numbers are not counted at all and which numbers occur in several counts).

The multiple of a number is a product of that number and another whole number. A factor is a number that a larger number can be divided by without leaving a remainder. To solve this problem, children will search for numbers with the most factors.

As it is necessary to keep counting past 10× each number, children may find a 100 square helpful to support counting in steps and recording results. Encourage them to place markers to show which numbers feature (for example, yellow counters on every second number, red counters on every third number and so on). There will be patterns to spot with each of these multiples.

## Try this

### Support

Initially limit the problem to counting in twos, threes, fours, fives and tens. Once children have mastered this, introduce further conditions.

### Extension

Encourage children to consider the properties of the nearly perfect planets in more detail. Is there a pattern to them? Planets with six factors between 2 and 100 are 60, 72 and 90. What do children notice about these numbers? Ask them to write rules for a nearly perfect planet (for example, must be even, must be a multiple of 3) and then to test their rules.

Challenge children to find rules to identify which planets are in which sequences. For example, multiples of 10 always end in a 0; the digits in multiples of 9 always add to make 9.

## Progress notes

Please use this space to make your own notes.

# 19 Coordinates and shapes

## Thinking starters

1 Look at this grid.

   a) Write down the coordinates of the points.

   A _____    B _____

   b) Mark points at:

   C (1,3)    D (4,5)

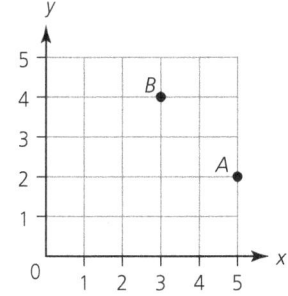

2 Three corners of a square are at (5,4), (2,1) and (5,1). What are the coordinates of the fourth corner? Draw the square on this grid.

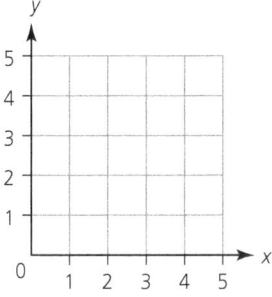

3 Three corners of a rectangle are at (1,3), (4,3) and (1,2). What are the coordinates of the fourth corner? Draw the rectangle on this grid.

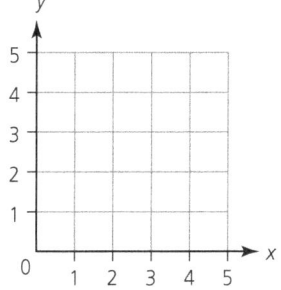

4 Draw a straight line on this grid between the points with coordinates (1,2) and (4,5). Write down the coordinates of two other points on the line.

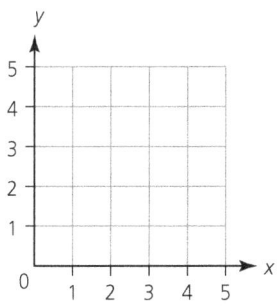

5 Draw a straight line on this grid between the points with coordinates (1,1) and (5,1). This line is one side of an isosceles triangle. Give two possible answers for the coordinates of the third vertex.

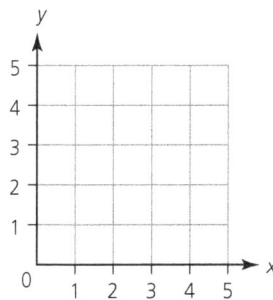

# Maths mastery

## Plotting pentagons

Tianna has been asked to plot the following points on a coordinate grid and join the points to make a pentagon.
- Can you help her?

(6,5)
(4,2)
(7,4)
(3,3)
(6,3)

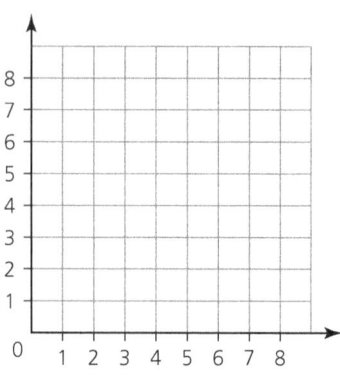

Daniel plots some coordinates and joins them up to form the vertices of a hexagon.
- What could the coordinates be?
- Draw an example with two of the coordinates at (1,8) and (8,1).

Show the method you used to solve the problem. Is it similar to or different from those used by your classmates?

### Support notes
Teach ways of remembering the order of coordinates; for example, the phrase 'along the hall, then up the stairs' is a useful way of reminding children that x-axis values should be written first. Another way is 'x is a cross' as in 'x is across'.

# Problem solving

**Reasoning skills**
- Spotting patterns and relationships
- Working systematically
- Making comparisons
- Using numerical reasoning

## Delivery drones

A pizza delivery company is using drones to deliver pizzas.

It sends out four drones at a time and flies them in a square shape. Sometimes their signal cuts out!

The pizza company needs to work out where the missing delivery drones are before the pizzas get cold.

Here, the signal of one of the drones has cut out. Can you tell where it is?

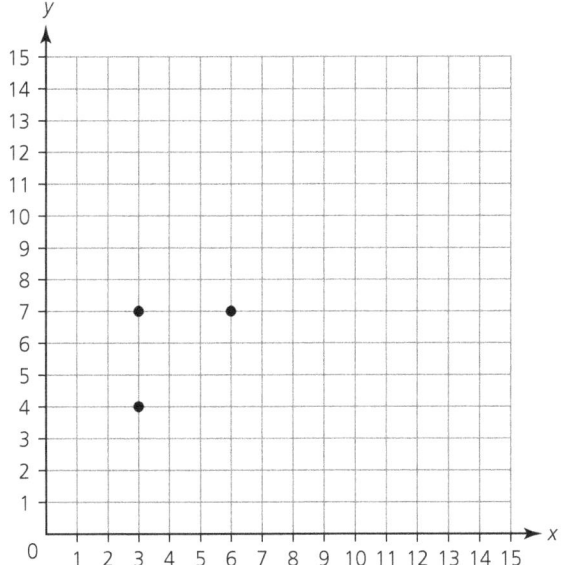

**Things to think about**
- How are grids used to show the position of shapes and objects?
- Explain how you can remember how to use coordinates correctly.
- How much information do you need to know what the square looks like?
- If these points are two corners of a square, **what else do we know?**
- Give me an **example** of a square that has (5,5) as one of its corners.
- **What do you notice** about the coordinates of the points of a square?
- **What is the same? What is different** about the coordinates of a square?

**Your challenge**

One day the signals of three of the drones cut out. The fourth drone is at point (5,5). What could the coordinates of the other drones be?

Look for patterns in the coordinates of each square you draw. What do you notice?

# Tips for success

Children investigate the coordinates of squares. They are asked to consider all the different squares possible when only one coordinate is given.

Children will practise the language of position and direction, particularly terms such as up, down, left, right, and coordinates, as well as using coordinates correctly. Children are expected to give coordinates in the first quadrant only, so only positive *x* and *y* values are needed.

Children should initially focus on drawing squares where each side of a square is either a horizontal or vertical line of equal length (they could later explore squares that are at an angle on the grid), so the coordinates of each corner are related. For example, a square may have corners (3,5), (3,9), (7,9) and (7,5).

Children should notice the repeated numbers in the coordinates; this is because each corner is level with each other. They should also notice that the difference between some of the numbers is the same: 7 is 4 more than 3, 9 is 4 more than 5 (because each side of a square is the same length). Children could begin to generalise and see patterns in each set of coordinates.

## Try this

### Support
Provide children with counters. Ask children to place a counter on point (5,5) on the grid. They should explore where they could put the counters to form different squares.

### Extension
Tell children that the drones are flying in a formation where the square is at an angle. Show examples of these on a grid:

Encourage them to look for patterns in the coordinates. How are the patterns similar to the squares with horizontal and vertical sides?

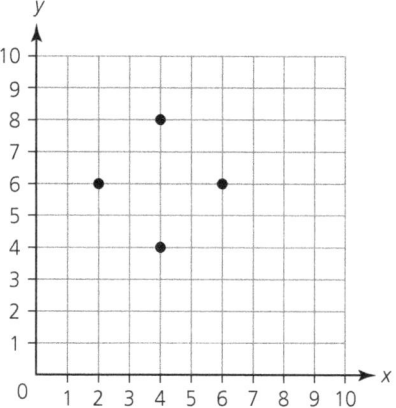

## Progress notes

Please use this space to make your own notes.

# 20 Fractions of amounts

## Thinking starters

1 Complete these.

   a) Shade $\frac{1}{4}$ of this bar.

   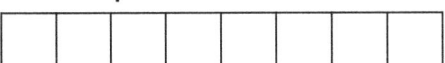

   b) Shade $\frac{1}{5}$ of this bar.

   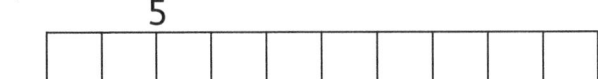

2 Answer these.

   a) Use this bar to find $\frac{3}{5}$ of 40.

   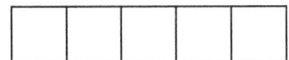

   b) Use this bar to find $\frac{5}{6}$ of 36.

   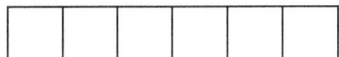

3 Complete these.

   a) $\frac{7}{10}$ of 30 = ☐

   b) $\frac{11}{12}$ of 24 = ☐

4 Answer these.

   a) A class has 30 children. $\frac{1}{6}$ of the children wear glasses.
      How many children wear glasses?

   b) Obe has 35 calculations for his homework. He has completed $\frac{3}{5}$.
      How many has he completed?

   c) In a class of 32 children, $\frac{5}{8}$ are girls. How many boys are in the class?

# Maths mastery

### Chocolate buttons

Mark takes $\frac{1}{4}$ of a packet of 40 chocolate buttons.

Lisa takes $\frac{3}{10}$ of a packet of 30 chocolate buttons.

- Who has more chocolate buttons? Convince me.

Show the method you used to solve the problem. Is it similar to or different from those used by your classmates?

### Support notes

Use 40 or 30 small objects such as counters or cubes to represent the 'whole' in each case and encourage children to practise physically splitting the whole into different fractions. Discuss how children might find unitary fractions of this amount: $\frac{1}{2}$, $\frac{1}{4}$ (Mark's number) and so on. Include 1/10. Once children have found what $\frac{1}{10}$ of 40 is, ask them what they need to do to find $\frac{3}{10}$ (Lisa's number).

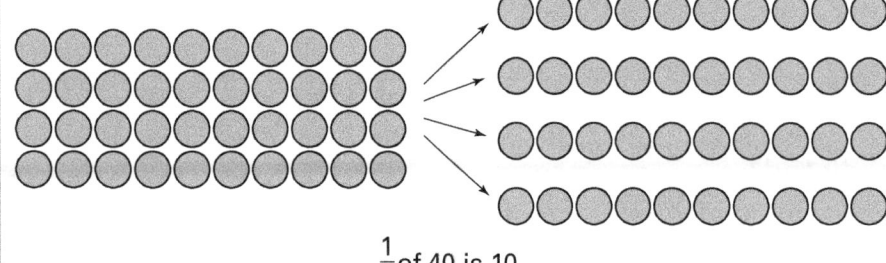

$\frac{1}{4}$ of 40 is 10

# Problem solving

**Reasoning skills**
- Spotting patterns and relationships
- Finding all possibilities
- Making connections
- Convincing

## It's a fraction of feet

Roy, the circus ringmaster, has got into a bit of a muddle! He can see a total of 64 feet and wheels in the circus ring.

He knows that $\frac{1}{4}$ of the feet belong to horses and that $\frac{1}{8}$ of the feet belong to acrobats.

Who could the other feet belong to?

The circus has at least one of each of these:
- horses with four feet
- dogs with four feet
- acrobats with two feet
- unicycles with one wheel
- clown's bicycle with two wheels.

**Things to think about**
- Can you work systematically to find all the different combinations of feet and wheels that total 64?
- Can you write all your combinations as fractions?
- Will you use 64 as the denominator or can you simplify the fractions?
- Can you use practical equipment to help you with your additions and your fractions?
- Give me an example of a combination of feet/wheels to total 64. **Another, another, another.**
- **Convince me** that you have found all the possible feet/wheel combinations.
- We know that the total number of feet and wheels is 64. **What else do we know?**

**Your challenge**
What animals, people or wheels might be in the circus ring?
Can you write each amount as fractions of the total?

# Tips for success

In this problem, children explore possible solutions for combinations of feet and wheels in a circus ring that will total 64. They then write these combinations as fractions of the whole amount.

Children may struggle with the concept of fractions of amounts. Explain that fractions are the proportion of a number or of a whole amount. All the fractions in this problem can be written using 64 as the denominator to show what proportion of 64 each amount is, for example $\frac{16}{64}$.

The fractions can also be expressed in their simplified form (for example, $\frac{1}{4}, \frac{1}{8}, \frac{1}{16}, \frac{1}{32}$) or as non-unit fractions (for example, $\frac{3}{16}, \frac{1}{32}$).

Children need to work systematically to ensure they find all possible combinations that total 64. They may start with the maximum number of dogs and minimum numbers of everything else, then reduce the number of dogs and increase the number of acrobats and so on.

Children may benefit from using practical apparatus (for example, interlocking cubes, counters or bead strings) to manipulate the different ways of totalling 64.

## Try this

### Support

Children may lose track of their addition part way through. Provide practical equipment such as interlocking cubes or counters. Give children 64 of each object so that the total they have to play with never changes. Then ask them to manipulate these to find different combinations of groups that total 64. Support those who may need additional help with recording fractions.

### Extension

Ask children to come up with their own combination questions using fractions. They could use the same context of a circus with animals and wheels but with different numbers or they could use a different context.

## Progress notes

Please use this space to make your own notes.

# 21 Symmetrical patterns

## Thinking starters

1. How many lines of symmetry does each shape have?

   a)   b)   c)   d)   e)

   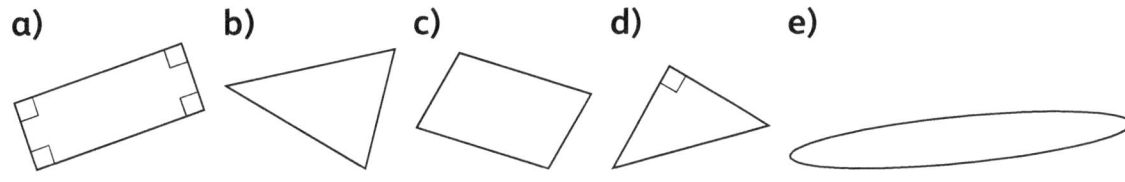

2. Anil says, 'A square has four lines of symmetry so a rectangle must have four lines of symmetry too.' Is Anil right? Explain your answer.

3. Dan says, 'The dotted line in this shape is a line of symmetry.'

   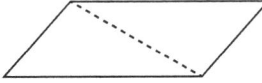

   Is Dan right? Explain your answer.

4. Lines of symmetry are always diagonals of shapes.

   Is this statement always, sometimes or never true?

5. Triangles have only 0 or 1 line of symmetry.

   Is this statement always, sometimes or never true?

6. The dotted line below is a line of symmetry.

   How many sides will the completed shape have?

# Maths mastery

## Symmetrical patterns

- Can you complete this pattern by shading 12 more of the small triangles, so that it has two lines of symmetry?

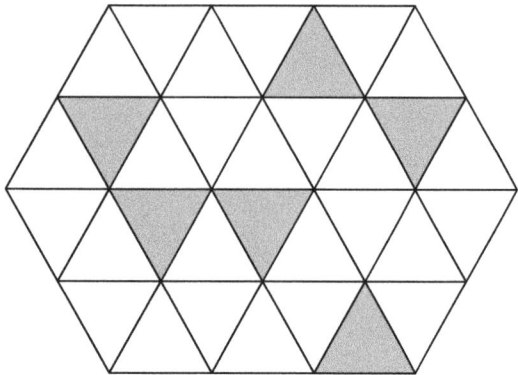

Look at this pattern.

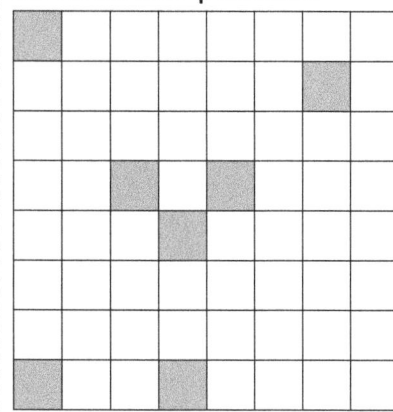

- Can you complete this pattern so that it has more than two lines of symmetry?

Show the method you used to solve the problem. Is it similar to or different from those used by your classmates?

### Support notes
Provide plastic (or card) equilateral triangles of two different colours. First, ask children to make the pattern as in the question, then slowly change the triangles as necessary in order to make the pattern symmetrical.

Children can use small mirrors to check that their pattern has two lines of symmetry once it is coloured in.

# Problem solving

**Reasoning skills**
- Finding all possibilities
- Working systematically
- Spotting patterns

## Flower symmetry

Mr Rake is designing a maths garden for children to use.

One of the features of the garden will be symmetrical rows of flowers. He has eight flowers to plant in a row: four blue flowers and four yellow flowers. The row will be symmetrical.

**Your challenge**
How many different symmetrical rows of flowers can you plant using four blue and four yellow flowers?

**Things to think about**
- Do you know what it means for something to be symmetrical?
- How could you model the different rows possible? You might like to draw each different coloured flower or use letters to represent them.
- How could you work systematically to make sure you have thought of all the possibilities?
- **What do you notice** about the way these flowers have been planted?
- Organise these flowers so that they are symmetrical. **Another, another, another.** Can you do this systematically?
- If you were asked to rearrange four cubes (two of each colour) in as many different ways as possible, how would this compare to the eight-flower problem you were asked? **What is the same? What is different?**

# Tips for success

Children investigate symmetrical patterns made by placing objects in a row (initially eight objects, four of each colour, but then extending to nine and then ten objects).

Symmetry is the property of a shape or pattern where one half is exactly the same as the other, as though reflected across a line.

A line of symmetry is a central line dividing a shape or pattern into reflected halves. Explain that lines of symmetry can exist in many directions (vertical, diagonal, horizontal) but, in this problem, children focus only on vertical lines of symmetry.

With the initial eight-flower problem, this is a vertical line between the fourth and fifth flowers. As the problem develops using different numbers of flowers, this vertical line of symmetry will change (odd numbers are interesting as the line of symmetry will need to go halfway through the middle flower).

Encourage children to work systematically (for example, making all possible designs beginning with a particular sequence of colours).

Children may notice that the challenge can be distilled to making different rows using four flowers (two of each colour) and then reflecting this to make a symmetrical eight-flower row.

Use mirrors as a support.

## Try this

### Support

Provide children who struggle with the concept of symmetry with a row of four cubes (two of each colour). Ask them to complete the row with another four cubes so that it becomes symmetrical.

Provide blue and yellow cubes or counters so children can model each possible row of flowers (and therefore can see if they have repeated any of their rows). They could photograph their rows to record what they have already done. Begin with a six-flower problem if it is helpful for children to start with fewer possibilities.

### Extension

Provide further arranging problems. For example, ask: *You have six cubes in a line, three blue and three green. How many different arrangements can you make?* Then ask: *How is this problem the same as the flower problem? How is it different?* Children may see that it is essentially the same problem. Ask them to change the problem so that it includes symmetry.

## Progress notes

Please use this space to make your own notes.

# 22 Number patterns

## Thinking starters

1 What is the next number in this sequence? Circle the correct answer.

   34     42     50     58     ☐

   a) 64          b) 65          c) 66

2 What is the rule for this sequence? Circle the correct answer.

   130    105    80    55    30

   a) −35         b) −25         c) +25

3 What is the missing number in this sequence? Circle the correct answer.

   1650    1600    ☐    1500    1450

   a) 1550        b) 1505        c) 1650

4 What is the missing number in this sequence? Circle the correct answer.

   2400    3400    4400    ☐    6400

   a) 4800        b) 5200        c) 5400

5 Find the rule and write the next two numbers in these sequences.

   a) 366    368    370    372    ☐    ☐    rule: ☐
   b) 1425   1420   1415   1410   ☐    ☐    rule: ☐
   c) 30     45     60     75     ☐    ☐    rule: ☐
   d) 9095   8095   7095   6095   ☐    ☐    rule: ☐

6 Write the missing numbers in these sequences.

   a) 318    418    ☐    618    ☐    818
   b) 95     ☐     91    89    87    ☐
   c) ☐     1200   1250   ☐    1350   1400
   d) 267    247    ☐    207    ☐    167

# Maths mastery

## Missing numbers

Sam has written some sequences.

| 30 | 39 | 48 | 57 | ☐ | ☐ | ☐ |
| 26 | 51 | 76 | 101 | ☐ | ☐ | ☐ |
| 130 | 240 | 350 | 460 | ☐ | ☐ | ☐ |
| 680 | 630 | 580 | 530 | ☐ | ☐ | ☐ |

- Can you work out what the next three numbers in each of Sam's sequences would be?
- Write anything you notice about each of the sequences.

---

- Is the number 55 in the sequence that starts −35, −20, −5, 10?
- How do you know?

Show the method you used to solve the problem. Is it similar to or different from those used by your classmates?

### Support notes

Use a blank number line to allow children to show each jump of the smaller numbers and then continue them. Encourage them to look at the patterns in the number sequences. Ask: *What do you notice?* within each sequence. So, for example, the ones digit in the first sequence goes down 0, 9, 8, 7, 6 ... and the tens digit in the final sequence repeats 80, 30, 80, 30 ...

# Problem solving

**Reasoning skills**
- Working systematically
- Finding all possibilities
- Making connections
- Spotting patterns and relationships

## Sequences of signs

Maurice Myner positions signs along motorways. Each sign has the same distance between it. Here, the distance in between is 50 miles.

One day, Maurice has a different set of five signs waiting for him.

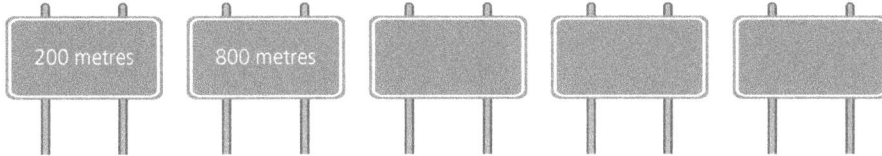

He can paint any number he wants on the three blank signs.

**Your challenge**

Find different sequences of five signs that include 200 and 800 metres. The 200 and 800 can go anywhere in the sequence of five.

What are the distances in between the numbers in your sequences?

**Things to think about**
- How could you represent the five motorway signs?
- Is there a way to approach this problem systematically?
- How might you record the different sequences of the five signs you think of?
- Arrange the numbers 200 and 800 into different number sequences. **What is the rule** for each sequence?
- **What is the link** between the numbers in this sequence: 200, 800, 1400, 2000, 2600?
- **What do you notice** about the number of possible sequences?

# Tips for success

Children explore different five-number sequences that have the numbers 200 and 800 in them (where the intervals between the five numbers are the same). Although the problem is set within the context of motorway signs, encourage children to consider negative numbers, even though they won't be seen on a motorway sign!

This investigation lends itself to a systematic approach. The obvious starting point is a sequence beginning with 200 and then followed by 800. As this will be a +600 sequence, the five numbers will be:

| 200 | 800 | 1400 | 2000 | 2600 | (+600) |

Encourage children to alter the position of the number 800:

| 200 | 500 | 800 | 1100 | 1400 | (+300) |
| 200 | 400 | 600 | 800 | 1000 | (+200) |

Some children may explore sequences where the number 200 is not the first number (this is particularly interesting as it often results in negative numbers):

| −400 | 200 | 800 | 1400 | 2000 | (+600) |

Another approach is for children to explore sequences that decrease rather than increase, for example:

| 800 | 600 | 400 | 200 | 0 | (−200) |

## Try this

### Support

Provide children with number lines to help work out each jump.

Take away the 'finding the rule' aspect of the investigation. Give them the rule and encourage them to find the sequence by placing the numbers in different positions.

### Extension

Encourage children to begin to consider what happens when the sequence continues below 0 and/or is a decreasing sequence.

## Progress notes

Please use this space to make your own notes.

# 23 Fractions and money

## Thinking starters

1  Complete these.

   a) $\frac{5}{7}$ of $35 = ☐

   b) $\frac{3}{8}$ of $32 = ☐

   c) $\frac{2}{5}$ of $45 = ☐

   d) $\frac{3}{4}$ of $56 = ☐

2  Find the missing amounts.
   Use the bars to help.

   a) $\frac{3}{4}$ of ☐ = $30

   b) $\frac{2}{3}$ of ☐ = $30

   c) $\frac{3}{5}$ of ☐ = $30

3  Answer these problems.

   a) Beth has $40. She saves $\frac{3}{5}$ of her money and spends the rest. How much did Beth save?

   b) Gus has taken some money on holiday. Gus says, 'I have spent $\frac{3}{4}$ of my money and I have $15 left.' How much money did Gus take on holiday?

   c) Tom has $\frac{2}{3}$ of the money that his sister Marion has. If Tom has $32, how much does Marion have?

# Maths mastery

### Fractions of money

Mark has been given $120 for his ninth birthday.

He has chosen to save $\frac{2}{5}$ of his money, to spend $\frac{1}{4}$ on clothes and to spend the rest on games for his tablet.

- How much money does he have left to spend on games?

Show the method you used to solve the problem. Is it similar to or different from those used by your classmates?

### Support notes

Use 120 small objects to represent the 'whole' and encourage children to practise physically splitting the whole into different fractions. Discuss how children might find unit fractions of this amount: $\frac{1}{2}, \frac{1}{4}$ and so on. Include $\frac{1}{5}$. Once children have found what $\frac{1}{5}$ of 120 is, ask them what they need to do to find $\frac{2}{5}$. Take both $\frac{2}{5}$ and $\frac{1}{4}$ away from the whole to find what is left.

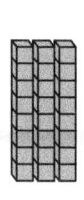 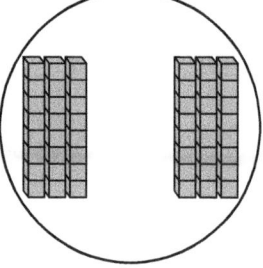 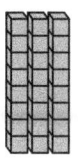 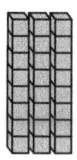

$\frac{1}{5}$ of 120 = 24

$\frac{2}{5}$ of 120 = 48

# Problem solving

**Reasoning skills**
- Solving problems
- Making connections
- Using numerical reasoning

## Mixed-up offers

Anthony went into a shop and tripped over, knocking all the price tags onto the floor.

The shop had a sale on and the price tags had two parts: the fraction, and the original price.

Using the price tags, you can work out the sale price.

Here are the parts to some of the price tags Anthony knocked over:

Anthony stood on two other price tags with his muddy feet:

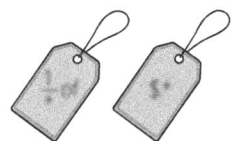

**Things to think about**
- How can you work out the sale price for each price tag?
- What could be the most expensive price tag Anthony knocked over? What could be the cheapest?
- How many different ways can you think of to make the number 24? How can you write this as a fraction of an amount?
- Suggest a price tag that you can make. **Another, another, another.**
- If $\frac{1}{4}$ of a price is $75, **what else do we know?**
- Give me **a hard and an easy** 'fraction of a price' problem.

### Your challenge

How many different price tags can you make using the first eight price tags shown?

Work out the sale prices for each price tag you make.

What numbers could be on the muddy price tags if the sale price is $24?

# Tips for success

In this problem, children are asked to use different parts of price tags (a fraction and a full price) to explore all possible prices in a sale.

This activity will help children practise the language of fractions, including numerator, denominator, half, quarter, three-quarters, eighths and five-eighths.

Children will already have experience of finding fractions of a discrete set of objects and will need to use these skills when finding fractions of prices.

To find a unit fraction of a price (that is, a fraction with 1 as the numerator), children first need to divide the price by the denominator. This splits it into equal parts. To find a non-unitary fraction of a price (that is, a fraction with a number other than 1 as the numerator, for example $\frac{3}{4}$ or $\frac{5}{8}$), they also need to multiply by the numerator to find the correct fraction. So, to find $\frac{3}{4}$, they divide by 4 (to give $\frac{1}{4}$) and then multiply by 3 (to give $\frac{3}{4}$).

Provide counting equipment such as base 10 apparatus or cubes to help children visualise and embed the process of finding fractions of amounts.

## Try this

### Support

Give children the same problem, but with unit fractions only ($\frac{1}{2}$, $\frac{1}{4}$ and $\frac{1}{3}$) as well as 2-digit prices that will give whole numbers ($36, $60, $12). Provide children with counting equipment to help find fractions of these numbers.

### Extension

Ask children to devise their own 'fraction of a price' problems for their peers to solve. Ask them to write a hard and an easy problem and ensure that they can work out the answer themselves before sharing it with peers.

## Progress notes

Please use this space to make your own notes.

# 24 Factors

## Thinking starters

1 Complete these.

   a) Write the missing factors of 32.

   1, 2, ☐, ☐, 16, 32

   b) Write the missing factors of 40.

   1, 2, ☐, ☐, ☐, 20, 40

2 Which of these numbers has the most factors?

   12, 16, 24 or 30

   How many factors does the number have?

3 Find all the factor pairs of:

   a) 12     b) 20     c) 32     d) 48

4 Write one number for each cell.

|  | Multiple of 5 | Not a multiple of 5 |
|---|---|---|
| Factor of 120 |  |  |
| Not a factor of 120 |  |  |

5 Tom says 7 is a factor of 63. Do you agree?

   Explain your reasoning.

# Maths mastery

## Factor pairs

Brianna is doing some calculations mentally.

She can use factor pairs to help her with some of them.

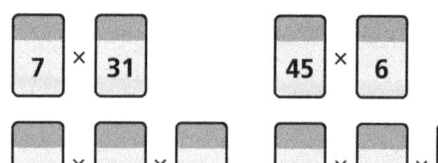

- Decide which calculations factor pairs would help with.
- Explain to Brianna how they could help.
- Explain why factor pairs will not help with the others.

Show the method you used to solve the problem. Is it similar to or different from those used by your classmates?

### Support notes

Provide children with plastic counters or cubes and encourage them to make as many different arrays as possible using them. For example, with 12 counters, they can make only three different arrays: 1 × 12, 2 × 6 and 3 × 4. Children can use their arrays to help identify the factors of each number.

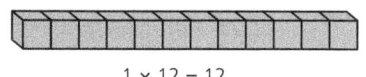
1 × 12 = 12

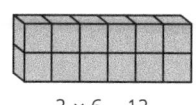
2 × 6 = 12

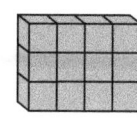
3 × 4 = 12

# Problem solving

**Reasoning skills**
- Working systematically
- Spotting patterns and relationships

## Pole position

When it is take-off time, everyone wants to be in the rocket's driving seat.

One crew thinks it has found a way to choose fairly who sits in the driving seat. They sit in a circle and spell the words POLE POSITION, pointing to each crew member for each letter. The person on whom the letter N falls sits in the driving seat.

**Things to think about**
- By spelling POLE POSITION, what are you actually doing in terms of numbers and counting?
- Can you think of a way to record who wins for different numbers of astronauts?
- Can you explain any of your answers or patterns?
- **What do you notice** about where the spelling chant ends?
- **What is the link** between the number of letters in the words and where the chant ends?
- If we know that the words POLE POSITION have 12 letters, **what else do we know?**
- **Convince me** that you can predict the best place to be for a counting chant.

**Your challenge**

If there are only two astronauts in the crew, how can you make sure that you get to sit in the driving seat?

What about four astronauts? Or six?

Try some odd numbers of astronauts.

# Tips for success

Children investigate how to choose someone to sit in the driving seat of a rocket using a counting chant. The chant is similar to the rhymes children use in the playground to choose who is 'it'. They should consider whether someone's position in the chant matters and/or whether it matters how many people are in the group.

Children will have the opportunity to practise division and recall factors of numbers when considering their results.

Through saying the chant with different group sizes, children will recognise that any group size which is a factor of 12 will result in the last person being in pole position (because there are 12 letters in POLE POSITION). Children may also recognise that, for numbers that are not a factor of 12, it is the remainder that is important; for example, for a group of 5, 12 ÷ 5 = 2 r2 so the end position is person 2.

Children can design a recording table to share results. For each group size, it needs to show the count and where it ends.

## Try this

### Support

Use counting equipment (coloured cubes/counters) to model each group size. Write the letters POLE POSITION on small cards so children can physically share them out (in order) according to the group size.

### Extension

Ask children to explore different chants to find whether they can spot a way to predict each 'best place to be' for different group sizes.

As a development, explain that the astronauts have changed the chant to 'I WANT THE COOL SEAT'. Without going through every possibility, in which group sizes would it be best to be in last place? Where would you stand if there were 13 in the group? Why?

## Progress notes

Please use this space to make your own notes.

# 25 Area of shapes

## Thinking starters

1 On this grid, each square represents a square centimetre (1 cm²).
   Find the area of each shaded shape.

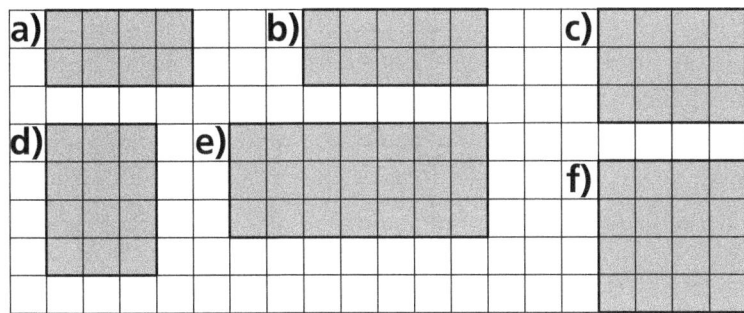

2 Josie has 12 centimetre squares. How could she arrange them into a rectangle?

3 A square has an area of 25 cm². What is the length of one of the sides?

4 In this rectangle, some squares have been shaded. What is the area of the whole rectangle?

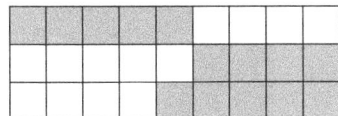

5 A square has sides of 7cm. What is the area of the square?

# Maths mastery

## Area and perimeter

Mary is working out the area and perimeter of a sequence of rectangles.

A 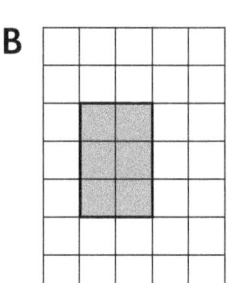 B 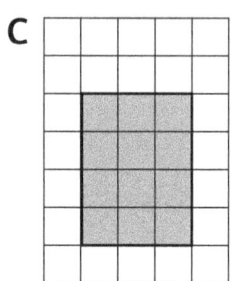 C D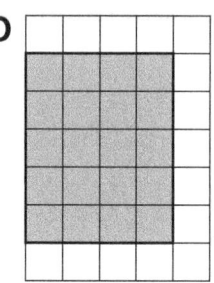

- Can you help her calculate the area and perimeter of these rectangles?
- Complete this table to show the results.

| Rectangle | Length (cm) | Width (cm) | Perimeter (cm) | Area (square cm) |
|---|---|---|---|---|
| A | 1 | 2 | 6 | 2 |
| B | | | | |
| C | | | | |
| D | | | | |
| | | | | |

- What do you notice?
- Can you predict the perimeter and area of the next rectangle, E, in the sequence?

Show the method you used to solve the problem. Is it similar to or different from those used by your classmates?

### Support notes
Encourage children to write on the shapes, counting and labelling each length. Once labelled, children can then add each side's length to calculate the total perimeter. In the same way, children can write numbers in each square to ensure that they count the area correctly. Children may realise that they are measuring an array and that all they need is the length and the width to work out the area.

# Problem solving

**Reasoning skills**
- Solving problems
- Making comparisons
- Using numerical reasoning

## Mr Shah's swimming pool shambles

Mr Shah lays tiles for swimming pools.

He uses a machine to cut tiled flooring to fit any shape of swimming pool that has straight lines and right-angled corners.

Today he has a problem. His machine is cutting pieces of flooring to the correct shape, but halving the dimensions of the actual swimming pool! For example:

The flooring cutter cuts this: □   for a pool with these dimensions:

The flooring cutter cuts this:   for a pool with these dimensions:

### Things to think about
- What is the area of a shape?
- If the length and the width of a shape are doubled, what happens to the area? Is this always true?
- What could you do to find out whether the smaller pieces will fit the larger swimming pool?
- Is 'the space inside a shape' a good **example** of 'the area of a shape'?
- **What is the link** between the area of a shape and an area of the same shape with double the dimensions?
- Draw **a hard and an easy** example of a shape that will fit four times inside a shape with double the dimensions.
- Is it **always, sometimes or never true** that four rectilinear shapes will fit together to make the same shape, but with double the dimensions?

### Your challenge

Mr Shah finds a way of using the pieces his machine cuts to fit the actual pool. What do you think he does?

Does this only work for squares and rectangles? Try some of these other shapes.

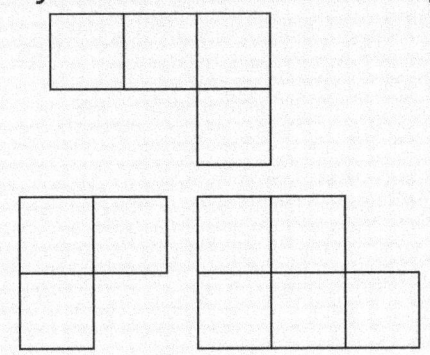

# Tips for success

Children use the context of swimming pool tiled flooring to investigate ways of making rectilinear shapes using smaller versions of the same shape, whose dimensions are half that of the original.

Children use the vocabulary of shape names (square, rectangle) and measure (length, width, area).

The area of a shape is the space within it. Children are expected to understand this concept but not to work it out using a formula. Instead they are encouraged to find the area by counting squares.

Children will find that they can make the flooring fit the pool shape by using four of the smaller pieces (that is, four 1 × 1 squares will fit a 2 × 2 square, four 1 × 3 rectangles will fit a 2 × 6 rectangle and so on). This works for other rectilinear shapes, although shapes will have to be rotated and flipped to fit together.

A common misconception is that, if a shape's dimensions are doubled, its area will also double. In fact, if a shape's length and width double, its area will quadruple. Shapes that triple their dimensions increase their area by nine times, shapes that quadruple their dimensions increase their area by 16 times and so on (these are all square numbers).

## Try this

### Support

Encourage children to investigate different squares and rectangles. Provide them with different squares and rectangles to cut out and use these shapes with centimetre-squared paper. Encourage children to put them together like a jigsaw before counting each square to find the area.

### Extension

Ask children to explore the link between the way a shape increases and the change in its area. They already know that doubling the length and width results in a quadrupling of the area. What happens if the shape's dimensions become three/four/five times as big? The pattern will be one of square numbers (see above).

As a further development, give children a limited number of squares (for example, six) and ask them to make as many rectilinear shapes as possible by putting the squares together (that is, each shape has an area of six squares). How many shapes can they find?

## Progress notes

Please use this space to make your own notes.

# 26 Calculation problems

## Thinking starters

1. Ben's car will cover 950 km on one tank of petrol. Ben drives 378 km and then 316 km. How many more kilometres could Ben drive without putting more fuel in the tank?

2. A stadium can hold 8570 people: 6715 are standing; the rest have seats. At a match, there are 356 empty seats. How many seats are taken?

3. Two numbers total 5000, but the difference is 2500. What are the two numbers?

4. Tom calculates:

   251 × 6 = 1201

   Show whether Tom is correct.

5. Find the missing numbers.

   ```
       ☐ 9 4
   ×     ☐
   ─────────
     3 5 4 6
   ```

6. Manisha works out:

   145 × 8 = 1160

   Explain how Manisha can use this to calculate 146 × 8.

7. Dev must calculate 360 × 8. He says, 'It would be easier to double 360 three times.'

   Show that Dev is right.

8. Dan has 45 counters. Ben has five times as many counters as Dan and Ali has three times as many counters as Ben. How many counters have they altogether?

# Maths mastery

## Missing digits

Some of the digits have been removed from these calculations.

- Can you work out what they are?

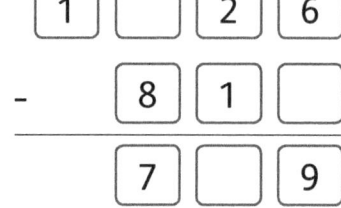

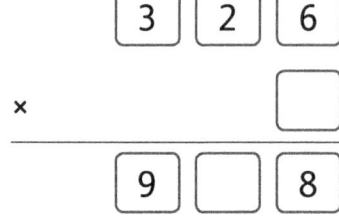

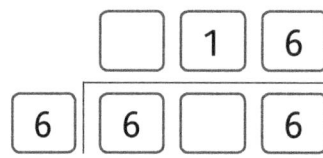

Show the method you used to solve the problem. Is it similar to or different from those used by your classmates?

### Support notes

Ensure that children are familiar and comfortable with these written methods. Encourage them to model each calculation using digit cards and, if they are unsure of a number, to try different digits until they find one that works. Further support can be provided by replacing the digit cards with place-value counters to gain an understanding of how the columns relate to each other and how this affects the steps in the calculation.

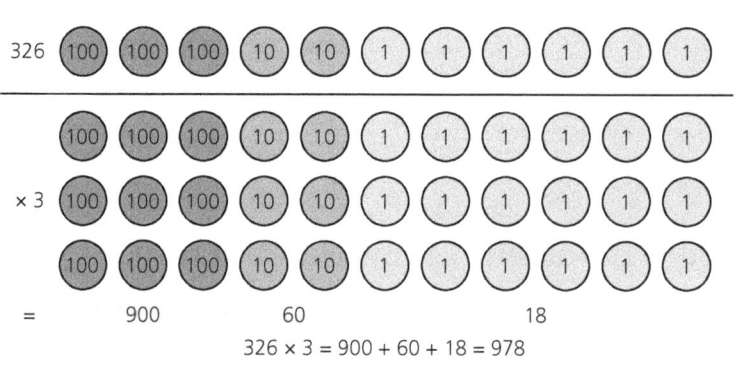

# Problem solving

**Reasoning skills**
- Solving problems
- Conjecturing and convincing
- Making connections
- Using numerical reasoning

## Mission multiply

A series of alien calculations has been found.

Look carefully at them:

1.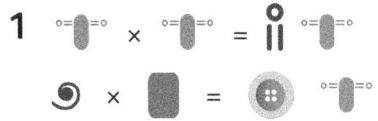

2.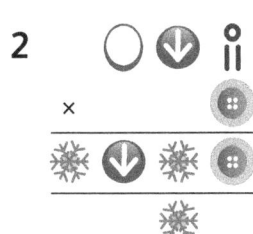

3. Clues: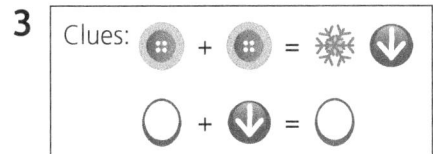

**Things to think about**
- How do you multiply a 3-digit number and a 1-digit number vertically?
- Can you make any statements about the numbers in the first multiplication?
- Can you see any parts of the multiplication that give a clue about what digits they are?
- The first multiplication is a square number. **What else do we know?**
- **Convince me** that the digits you have chosen for each symbol are the correct ones.
- Can you write your own **hard and easy** symbol problems? What makes them more difficult or easier?

**Your challenge**

Think carefully about the digit that each symbol could represent.

Find as many different multiplications as you can that fit each calculation.

Some may have one; some may have several.

As you work through the multiplications, you may change your answers!

# Tips for success

Children explore different multiplications that could be represented by a set of symbols. They should use their knowledge of both multiplication table facts and vertical multiplication to find different multiplications that fit the given symbols. The formal written layout for multiplying a 3-digit number by a 1-digit number is where both numbers have been written vertically. The numbers are multiplied column by column from right to left. In this particular example, there are two addition clues to help children work out the missing digits in the calculation.

Children should be encouraged to explore ideas initially and then begin to make numerical observations about the digits (for example, the first multiplication shows the same digit multiplied by itself, resulting in a number that ends with that same digit again. The only square numbers that obey this rule are 5 × 5 = 25 and 6 × 6 = 36 so these are the two possible answers). Ask: *What else do we know about the digits in the third multiplication?* Children may find the two additions helpful in giving clues (for example, in the second clue, the second digit must be 0: when it is added to a symbol, the symbol stays the same). Provide further time for exploring possible multiplications. The symbol values are as follows:

⬇ = 0  ❄ = 1  ◯ = 2  ⁚ = 3

⬤ = 5  ▮ = 6  ☽ = 7 (or 8)  ▮ = 8 (or 7)

## Try this

### Support
Practise multiplication table facts by giving children a fairly open-ended multiplication to investigate (for example, give them the second multiplication, without the first to limit it). Children could fill in a multiplication square and use their answers to find numbers easily.

### Extension
Ask children to develop their own multiplication symbol challenges, checking that they give just enough clues for others to be able to work out the answer. Introduce the idea of aliens using one symbol to represent an entire number. This is a pre-algebra concept and children should be able to understand it. Ask children to write their own number sentences using 'human' numbers and one 'alien' number, for example 9 × ◊ = 108. Children work in pairs to decide how to find the alien numbers.

## Progress notes
Please use this space to make your own notes.

# 27 Finding different possibilities

## Thinking starters

1 Write all the pairs of whole numbers that add to make 15.
   How do you know you have got them all?

2 The difference between a pair of two-digit numbers is 13.
   What could the pair of numbers be? Write three possible answers.

3 A restaurant menu has four different choices for the main course. There are five choices for dessert. How many different meals of main course and dessert can you order?

4 Jo has three number cards. She uses them to make numbers.

   | 3 | 4 | 2 |

   How many two-digit numbers can Jo make?
   Write them in order from smallest to largest.

5 Find three different ways of completing:

   ☐☐ × ☐ = 252

6 My age is a multiple of 8. Next year my age will be a multiple of 7. How old am I?

7 A farmer has cows and chickens on the farm. Altogether the animals have 24 legs. How many cows and chickens could there be on the farm?

# Maths mastery

## Outfit challenge

Mark has three different tops and two different pairs of jeans.

- How many different outfits could Mark make from these clothes?
- What if Mark had three different pairs of jeans?
- What if Mark included four different T-shirts to go with his three tops and three pairs of jeans. How many different combinations could there be?

Show the method you used to solve the problem. Is it similar to or different from those used by your classmates?

### Support notes

Children can model this problem using (for example) combinations of coloured cubes. However, it is important that they then relate their findings to a multiplication. One way of doing this is for children to place their combinations of cubes in an imaginary multiplication grid. They will then notice the multiplication calculation needed to solve the problem.

2 (jeans) × 3 (tops) = 6 combinations

# Problem solving

**Reasoning skills**
- Solving problems
- Working systematically
- Finding all possibilities
- Using numerical reasoning

## Revenge of the creepers

An intergalactic gardener has been asked to report back to Earth about what is growing in her space station greenhouse. Two types of plants are growing there:

1 The Ziggle plant is a harmless creeper, good for providing shelter and its leaves taste delicious in a salad.

2 The Zorgon plant is a carnivorous creeper. Astronauts shouldn't get too close to it if they want to keep their fingers!

Unfortunately, both plants look the same. The only way to tell them apart is to count their leaves.

Ziggles have three leaves and Zorgons have four.

**Your challenge**

The gardener counts 62 leaves altogether.

How many Ziggle and how many Zorgon plants could there be?

**Things to think about**
- What is the difference between the Ziggle and Zorgon plants?
- If the gardener counts eight leaves, which plants are in the greenhouse? What about 12 leaves?
- Can you use exchange methods to find a different combination? For example, four Ziggles have the same number of leaves as three Zorgons. Does this help?
- Give me an **example** of a number that is a multiple of both 3 and 4.
- What is the **quickest or easiest** way to find out whether a number is a multiple of 3 or 4?
- **What is the same? What is different** about multiples of 3 and multiples of 4?
- 60, 36, 15, 12, 24. Which is the **odd one out**?
- **What is the link** between the number of Ziggles and Zorgons that there could be in the greenhouse?

# Tips for success

Children are presented with a greenhouse containing 62 leaves and two possible plants that might be growing there (one with three leaves, the other with four). They investigate combinations of multiples of 3 and 4 that equal 62.

A multiple of a number is the result of multiplying that number by another whole number. Children will practise multiples of 3 and 4 and explore combinations of those numbers. Some children may initially take a trial-and-improvement approach, choosing a multiple of 3 and seeing whether there is a multiple of 4 that will equal 62 when combined with it. Others may try drawing the plants or use counting equipment as a support.

A systematic way to find all the possibilities is to start with one type of plant each time and gradually see whether it is possible. A table could be used to collate results and reveal patterns. A table may begin as follows:

| No. of Ziggle plants | No. of Ziggle leaves | No. of leaves remaining | No. of Zorgon plants | Combinations |
|---|---|---|---|---|
| 1 | 3 | 62 – 3 = 59 | Not possible | |
| 2 | 6 | 62 – 6 = 56 | 56 ÷ 4 = 14 | 2 Ziggles and 14 Zorgons |
| 3 | 9 | 62 – 9 = 53 | Not possible | |

## Try this

### Support

Simplify the problem so children are asked to find possible combinations of Ziggles and Zorgons where there is a total of 32 leaves. Provide counting equipment (for example, cubes) for children to model each set of plants.

### Extension

Encourage children to explore what happens when the number of leaves changes: *See how many combinations of plants you can find if there are 75 leaves overall.* Or if the type of plant changes: *See how many combinations you can find if one plant has 4 leaves and the other has 6.*

Children could create their own similar problems for peers to solve. For example, a number of planets: some with 4 moons, some with 5. How many combinations of planets could they find if there are 67 moons visible?

## Progress notes

Please use this space to make your own notes.